Praise for Resurrecting

"*Resurrecting Anthony* is a true story that wil
heart forever. Amidst the worst of crisis, Tony and Linda never lose
sight of the fact that life is a gift—an important lesson for others
facing challenge and maybe even more importantly, for those of us
taking our day-to-day lives for granted. I loved this book."
> —Keith Ferrazzi, #1 *NYT* best-selling author of
> *Who's Got Your Back* and *Never Eat Alone*

"Powerful lessons in letting go, being present, failure, belief, goals,
perseverance, and making the toughest of decisions—expressed in a
way that can only be shared by parents who have eighteen months
to save their child. It's a story I shared last night around the dinner
table with our own children. Thank you Linda and Tony for this
honest account of your family's journey with your son."
> —Verne Harnish, author of *Mastering the
> Rockefeller Habits*

"I want to thank you for the gift of your words in *Resurrecting
Anthony*. You touched me on every level. Yours is a love story as
deep and rough and terrible and joyous as there is. Where did your
strength come from? How did you not stop, not give up, not quit?
Powered by love—that I know."
> —Tom Redmond, Redmond Group, Inc.

"Thank you from the bottom of my heart for personally inviting
me into your family and your world, and into the "depth of your
souls." I am honored and feel privileged to have read this heart-
breaking, yet relentlessly inspiring story. Linda and Tony, you have
done a brilliant job in weaving your innermost and vulnerable parts
of your world for me to experience, and for all readers to experience
the roller coaster ride of your life ... the good and the unbearable."
> — Nancy Lorenzano, Ph.D.,
> The Lorenzano Group

"*Resurrecting Anthony* is inspirational. It made me choke back tears. It made me renew my commitment to be a more dedicated professional educator. It made me renew my focus to be a better husband, a more patient father, and a more caring grandfather. Indeed, it left me with an overwhelming sense of humility. It made my worst days seem mundane and trivial."

— Glenn Alexander, Superintendent of Clermont County Ohio Educational Service Center

"*Resurrecting Anthony* is an unforgettable story of turning tragedy into triumph. Tony and Linda Cole's unyielding determination in the face of adversity will resurrect your courage!"

—Roger Crawford, author *How High Can You Bounce?* and *Think Again!*

"*Resurrecting Anthony* touched my heart. Not because of the pain and emotion that he and his family have experienced, but because of the lessons he teaches all of us. Know what really matters; accept everyone; find joy at being in the present and remember that every day is a gift."

—Walt Gerano, Independent Consultant

"*Resurrecting Anthony* is a source of power and inspiration for everyone. It is a story that opens your eyes and heart to the fragility of life and the reality that, in a blink of an eye, life can change forever. You feel the dedication, acceptance and love of a devastated family and their courage to face reality. *Resurrecting Anthony* will help you appreciate, accept and value every minute of your life."

—Ralph Pim, author *Perfect Phrases for Coaches* Associate Professor & Director of Competitive Sports, Department of Physical Education United States Military Academy at West Point

"Life changed forever for the Cole family the day their son Anthony suffered from a life threatening heart condition. This is a powerful story of love and courage. Through every setback and emotional challenge, Tony and Linda demonstrated an unwavering inner strength and passion necessary to bring their son home!"

– J. Paul Brophy, author of *Zero to Sixty in 9 Years*

"*Resurrecting Anthony* was so inspiring I couldn't put the book down! "Celebrating Anthony" would have been an appropriate title, too. Anybody who was a kid, has a kid, or wants a kid will find more meaning per page than you can get from any book on parenting. People throw around the term "life's too short" without any concept of how true that can be and your story paints a picture of the term with an exclamation point."

> — Dave Kurlan CEO, Objective Management
> Group, Inc.

"'Eventually God spoke to me. Anthony is going to make it. But there will be a price.' These words set the tone for a sensitive and beautifully written account of the journey taken by Linda and Tony Cole in dedicating their lives to supporting and rehabilitating their son Anthony. From my role as a district support person I had the privilege across time of seeing and experiencing their commitment to establishing goals, setting priorities, and ensuring that if they couldn't "fix" Anthony, they could continue to create joy and provide quality of life. As shared, "To live in this particular moment in time, to focus on loving and connecting with those important before they are taken from us, or we from them ... perhaps that is Anthony's lesson for us all."

> — Laurel Frank, District Support, Sycamore
> Community Schools

"An inspiring book for anyone who is experiencing crisis in their lives. *Resurrecting Anthony* offers us hope, teaches us to never give up, and shows how to summon the courage from within to conquer our challenges. Most importantly, this 'must read' book reveals that no matter what you are experiencing you are not alone. A truly heartbreaking and motivational story."

> — Aleta St. James, author of *Life Shift*

"*Resurrecting Anthony* is a story that will touch any parent. Linda and Tony Cole walk us through the anguish and small triumphs that redefined their lives. It's raw and unblinking in its honesty, pain and tenderness. Discover what this family came to realize: there may not always be an apparent reason, but there is always a way through tragedy."

> — Anita Williams, Co-founder, Imagination
> Works, Inc., author of *60 Second Referral*

"An unsparingly honest log of a father's life after his son undergoes a cruel brain injury. If this family can survive and stay upright, you can do anything."
— Victoria Moran, author of
Creating a Charmed Life

"*Resurrecting Anthony* is not just the story of Anthony's brain injury and rehabilitation. It's the story of the journey traveled by Tony and Linda as they changed directions and grew as individuals and as a couple. Every time I wave to Anthony as he is being wheeled by our house, I am inspired by his resilience and determination, and by the Cole family's courage to dream a new dream. Every teacher and every parent who faces life with a child with a disability should read this book!"
— Karen A. Matuszek, Coordinator of
Special Education Services –
Archbishop Moeller High School

"*Resurrecting Anthony* greatly expanded my awareness of my heart and soul. It gave me the gift of greater appreciation, and more commitment to what I value most. I experienced light beamed deep into remote parts of my consciousness, often bouncing on my conscience; leaving me resolved to change some of my own behaviours."
— Paul O'Kelly, Founding Partner of
O'KellySutton, Offaly, Ireland

"*Resurrecting Anthony* is beautifully written and very insightful. I recommend this book to anyone dealing with a child with special needs or who has been faced with traumatic circumstances beyond their control. Being a mother of a child with Autism, this book helped me see that men and women process loss and emotions differently. I know God will use this book to help bring families together, to help restore marriages and to help health care professionals like myself understand the obstacles that our patients and families often face."
— Rhonda Fecher, RN, Children's Hospital
Medical Center

RESURRECTING
ANTHONY

A True Story of
COURAGE *&* DESTINATION

LINDA COLE *&* TONY COLE

Alexandra
Publishing LLC

First edition

Book cover and interior design by Barbara Aronica-Buck

Published by Alexandra Publishing, LLC
P.O. Box 42122, Cincinnati Ohio 45242
Phone:513-376-8782
Fax: 513-791-3468
www.ResurrectingAnthony.com

Library of Congress Cataloging in Publication
Cole, Linda 1956-
Resurrecting anthony: a true story of courage and destination / Linda Cole and
Tony Cole.
Summary: "The true, inspiring story of triumph over tragedy, which documents
the Cole family's devotion and determination to rehabilitate their son, Anthony,
who suffered a heart attack and brain damage at the age of twelve. The family sum-
mons the inner strength to make hard decisions, the courage to do what must be
done and the courage to accept a new life and family." —Provided by publisher.
1. Inspiration 2. Self help. 3. Parenting. 4. Health. 5. Family. 6. Biography.
I. Cole, Tony, 1955-
2010923903

ISBN 978-0-9843226-0-2

10 9 8 7 6 5 4 3 2 1

Printed in the United States of America

"A little lantern can do
what the great sun can never do—
it can shine in the night."

—AUTHOR UNKNOWN

DEDICATION

To the many wonderful people we have been blessed with since
September 8, 1998, people we might never have known.
Each nurse, therapist, aide and special education teacher who
has worked with Anthony over the years has brought a different
and useful perspective, along with their treasured individual person-
ality, to his case and ultimately to our household. It is only with
their kind and constant vigilance that we have managed
Anthony's health, well-being and happiness.

ACKNOWLEDGMENTS

On the cover of any book is written the authors' names, but clearly a team effort brings the title to fruition. To Eleanor Dugan, whose early mentoring and coaching set us on our way. To Rob Seal, whose enthusiasm helped us get to square one. To John Kachuba, for his patient direction and editing. To Barbara Aronica-Buck, whose interest in our story is clearly demonstrated in the cover design of the book and series, and in the details of the layout. To Peggy Linneman, for her commitment to creating the ideal Personal Courage Series® logo. To David Rippe, for his nurturing through the long and lonely writing process, for his expertise which led us through the difficult maze of book publishing and marketing, and for his belief in *Resurrecting Anthony*, The Personal Courage Series® and The Business Courage Series®. To my cousin, Kim Costa Walters, whose time and energy ensured that this story, one which she knew intimately from her own personal experience, was proofread to perfection. And finally to our sister, Jeni, whose constant presence in our lives offered much needed support and encouragement to write *Resurrecting Anthony* and to stay the course.

Congratulations on a job well done.

INTRODUCTION

Many years ago I read a mother's philosophical approach to her child's brain injury and the resulting drastic changes in her life. She likened her experience to "ending up in Germany when she had always planned to visit Italy." The implication was that she was in a foreign land and that she was okay with it, even though it wasn't what she had hoped.

When we found ourselves, as parents, suddenly confronting unbelievable heartache and hardship after our twelve-year-old son, Anthony, suffered a heart attack and subsequently brain damage, we were unprepared. Prior to that, Anthony had been healthy and vibrant with a life of unlimited potential ahead of him. And then, tragedy struck. We had no experience, no formal coping skills or training to anticipate and deal with the newly acquired physical, emotional and financial burdens that followed. The toll it took on us was far reaching, life changing, affecting every aspect of our existence. Even today we are coming to terms with events that began nearly twelve years ago.

But we continue to persevere. Why? What was it that

allowed us to find our way through our personal "dark night of the soul" toward brighter days? Why did we make it through when so many in similar situations give up? How did our business grow in the midst of the untold grief and sorrow? Why did our marriage survive when so many fail under the weight of such tragedies?

A large percentage of families are broken as a result of child tragedies like the one we have experienced. A nurse once told me that 85% of marriages don't make it. Sadly the divorce rate among this segment of the population is higher than that of the general population, and yet the need for love, support and teamwork is much greater. In many cases, the family dynamic becomes so strained that it causes one parent, usually the father, to separate, thus leaving the mother to raise the healthy children, care for the sick or injured one, navigate between doctor and therapy appointments and the myriad of details involved in a medically complicated child, all while holding a job. The reality of this scenario is heart breaking. Everyone involved loses.

While we both experienced the emotional roller coaster of hope and despair that coincided with this tragic reality, we recognized that *Resurrecting Anthony* could potentially have more impact if told from a male perspective. Our hope, in writing this book through Tony's viewpoint, is to help parents figure out how they might adapt in difficult circumstances and commit to keeping their families together. Thus I have written and crafted this book through personal experience and observation, business writings and notes from Tony. Not an easy task, but one we hope will offer useful strategies while demonstrating how parents might work through the worst of times together, how things can get better and how a new family unit, healthy and intact, can eventually emerge from the ashes.

Looking back, there were many factors that allowed us to muddle through, to soldier on, until we came to the place we are today. To be sure it was a difficult journey—one that had many detours, pitfalls, roadblocks and false steps. Certainly our faith in God and our faith in His vision of our family carried us through the tough times. The legion of caregivers was a huge blessing. And the incredible support of our family cannot be overstated. Nor can the amazing contributions of our friends and business associates. Truly, we were fortunate to have the support, resources, intelligence and faith to endure.

Twelve years on however, there is one telling trait that has become clear, one that we are certain can be found inside the millions of others who also have made it through the unfortunate crises that inevitably occur. That one telling trait is courage. The courage to summon the inner strength to make hard decisions. The courage to listen to your intuition. The courage to stand up to authority figures who might be smarter than you. The courage to say, "No, this is not right." The courage to commit to the people you love. And finally, most importantly, the courage to accept a new life and, in our case, a new family.

This realization about courage led us to write *Resurrecting Anthony*. It is not an easy story to tell. The memories are painful; our emotions still sensitive. The act of revealing the intimate details of our personal lives is daunting. But, we found the courage to tell it because we believe there is value in sharing our story with others. We do so in the hope that those in crisis will learn how to cope, how to be open and accepting of offered help, and how to advocate for needed services. We hope to inspire people to summon the courage they need to persevere, to commit without reservation, to adapt. We hope that others might learn from our mistakes and gain from our progress.

Life is unpredictable. Circumstances occur in unexpected ways at unexpected times. And despite your best efforts, nothing completely prepares you for the dire situations you encounter. You can take CPR training. You can buckle your seatbelt to keep yourself safe on the road. You can install an alarm system to keep your home and family secure.

You can do all these things and more, and they may reduce the risk that something bad may happen in your life. But the unfortunate reality is that tragedy will still find you. It is inevitable.

The question is: How will you respond when the crisis strikes? Will you let life's challenges best you? Do you have the courage to persevere? Or will you allow fear and despair to defeat you?

When we speak of courage we are not talking about the bravery of a soldier putting him or herself in harm's way—though clearly the men and women of the Armed Services are courageous. But we are speaking about the courage it takes to face your personal obstacles and setbacks whatever they may be.

Courage is doing what you have to do, even if you dread every minute of it. Courage is forcing your self to get out of bed each morning to meet the obstacles and frustrations head on. It is putting one foot in front of the other—day after day after day. Courage is swallowing hard and confronting the challenges. It is opening your mind to new places, new possibilities. Courage is finding the energy to stay the course, or to alter the course, if you know in your heart, that you must.

Courage can be painful and tedious. It requires that you dig deep inside to find the guts to carry on. To find the drive and the belief that you can overcome or adapt.

That is what led us to write this book and to develop The

Personal Courage Series.® While your individual circumstance is unique to you, thousands if not millions, of others have experienced similar tragedy—and they have made it through. You are not alone. There is hope. By learning from the experiences of others and calling upon similar resources you can perhaps shorten the time it takes to rebound, or reduce the emotional pain and turmoil involved.

We believe that this book, *Resurrecting Anthony*, and The Personal Courage Series® will demonstrate how many have overcome obstacles, dealt with chronic illnesses, suffered tragedies and continued to thrive and grow—and even found happiness again—so that you might do the same.

Can you find the will, the determination and the courage to conquer your fears and overcome your challenges? And when you find yourself in Germany instead of Italy, will you summon the courage to adapt? To learn the language? To enjoy the culture? I truly hope that you will, because while these two places are distinctly different, "Germany" has many wonderful assets you would never have imagined.

Warmest regards,
Linda Cole

CHAPTER 1

Pinnacle Club

BOCA RATON, FLORIDA
MAY 13, 2000

Last December it seemed like a great idea to put together an inspirational message that my son, Anthony, and I would present at the annual USI Insurance Services top producer conference. But, as I stood behind the curtain waiting for the cue that said I was on stage, I was less certain.

I heard the emcee introduce me: *"Many, maybe most of you, know this man. If you don't know him personally, I'm sure you have heard of him. For the last two years he has worked closely with several of our offices throughout the country."*

As I listened to these words, I looked back. Oh, how hard the last twenty months had been. It was now a little over a year and a half since my son, Anthony, had suffered a heart attack. The lack of oxygen during resuscitation had left him in a coma for months. Since September 8, 1998, each day had been a struggle.

"He has driven these organizations to perform better, resulting in increased sales and higher margins. He has given these offices a different vision of what selling is and can be."

1

My personal ups and downs had clearly followed Anthony's medical condition, resulting in my less than adequate personal and professional performance along the way. My emotional roller-coaster had made home life hard on those I loved. I was certain there were moments that the stress had spilled over to affect a training session.

"He has coached individual producers in each of these offices to accomplish what they never thought possible, helping them understand that our lives are shaped not only by our abilities, but by our attitude and conduct."

Somehow, I had managed to help these organizations move forward, even while I had struggled to do this in my own life. I felt a flash of pride that was quickly doused by disappointment in my own ability to come to terms with life's recent challenges.

"Here to 'Ignite the Fire Within' is Tony Cole of Anthony Cole Training Group."

The key to the presentation is the acronym S.P.A.R.K. The "S" stands for Specific Goals—having a clear destination for life and established goals to measure your progress toward that destination. The "P" stands for Passion—building desire for success and committing to do everything possible to succeed. The "A" stands for Action—doing the necessary things that move you toward your goals. The "R" stands for Responsibility—taking ownership of results and maintaining an even keel relative to your outlook toward business and personal challenges.

The "K" stands for Kaizen, which is a Japanese term that means constant, incremental and never ending improvement. The "K" is the crucial letter in this acronym and this is where Anthony's story enters the presentation.

We kept Anthony secreted away in a room nearby waiting for the signal to be stage side.

As I finished defining Kaizen, I began: "Anthony was born on August 4, 1986 …" Slides of my son prior to his cardiac arrest appeared on the projector behind me.

"He was a quiet, unassuming kid, polite and well liked by nearly everyone. As a baby, he was obsessed with—basketballs, footballs, soccer balls, baseballs—any kind of ball. Over the years he became an accomplished athlete, playing tight end for a champion junior league football team. He pitched a no-hitter at the age of ten, and was an all-star catcher for a winning baseball team. But his passion was basketball. He played junior league from the time he was seven, practiced his shots everyday on the driveway and was on the court during recess regularly. An avid fan of the Chicago Bulls, his idol was Michael Jordan and his dream was to be a professional basketball player.

"On September 8, 1998, as Anthony was joining a game during recess at the Sycamore Junior High School, he fell to the playground unconscious."

Pictures of him at Children's Hospital and shots from the last twenty months appeared in succession. The slide show stopped at a photo of Anthony sitting in his wheelchair, head cocked, smiling gently at the camera.

CHAPTER 2

Anthony is Airlifted

SEPTEMBER 8, 1998

As Linda and I returned to the office from lunch, the phone rang. When I answered it, a woman, identifying herself as an employee from the junior high school, breathlessly told me that something had happened to Anthony. She instructed me to go immediately to Children's Hospital Emergency Room. I pressed her for details, thinking maybe he had broken an arm or fallen and cut himself, but she said she didn't have any information, only that he was being airlifted from the playground by helicopter. Airlifted! The word jolted me. My stomach knotted. A rush of fear overwhelmed me. I called to Linda, yelling that something had happened to Anthony and that we needed to leave immediately.

We sped to Children's Hospital, frantically discussing what could have happened to our son that would require an airlift. I called Sycamore Junior High School en route and was told that Anthony had needed resuscitation, paramedics had responded to their emergency call, and that the helicopter was still on the playground.

I pressed the accelerator and dialed 911, hoping to let authorities know that we were going to break the speed limit in our haste to cover the twenty miles that separated us from the hospital. The operator's response was curt, and I disconnected within seconds, shifting my focus to navigating in and out of traffic on the I-71 Interstate like a Grand Prix driver. The mystery of what had happened to Anthony and my frustration at not knowing current goings-on escalated my normally impatient driving habits into outright aggression as we rocketed south.

By the time we ran into the emergency room two chaplains approached us. No nurses, no doctor, just the two chaplains. They were expecting us.

The chaplains took us to a small consultation room furnished with soft lighting and seating. One of them asked about our religious affiliation. I replied that we were Catholic. The other chaplain produced a Bible and asked us to pray. Pray? Pray for what? We wanted to see our son and make sure he was okay. We wanted to see him now. Was this conference really necessary? I sensed, in a remote and logical corner of my mind, that the question about our religious leanings was significant. One of the chaplains informed us that Anthony hadn't arrived and asked us to be patient, telling us that we might not be able to see him immediately. Patience wasn't a virtue that either Linda or I had at that moment. The glass doors slid open.

We hurried out of the consultation room to see emergency personnel rush Anthony in. He was lying on a steel gurney, covered by a sheet and tethered, but writhing. His eyes were open, unfocused, his face smeared with blood, and he was making unintelligible noises. A breathing tube jutted out of his throat. An IV connected his arm to a bag. EMTs surrounding him were

suddenly joined by several doctors and nurses as they rushed past us into the emergency area. We called out to Anthony, letting him know we were there, but were unable to tell if he recognized us. We stood by helplessly, trying to peer over shoulders and between arms, as the emergency team worked on our son in the ER bay.

Within an hour, Anthony was moved to intensive care, into a room like all the others surrounding a central nursing station, with a glass front that allowed medical personnel to visually supervise each patient as well as monitor their status remotely.

Anthony was now heavily sedated. His eyes were swollen shut and the left side of his face was an angry, open wound. There were burn marks on his chest where the EMTs had used the defibrillator paddles in multiple attempts to jumpstart and stabilize his heart. The only good news was that he had started to breathe on his own, so the breathing tube had been removed.

Because I had never experienced a major medical emergency, I didn't understand what was happening around me. My mind didn't have a folder of prior experience to reference so it was unable to point to any logical sequence of events upon which I might depend for guidance. I was completely caught off guard.

Dazed, Linda and I listened to doctors and nurses talk about the event, about Anthony's current condition, about future tests, but so much of it was like a foreign language to us. We listened, not comprehending most of the words, nodding and asking questions that we hoped might translate into something they could understand. All the while we stared at our son who had become a receptacle for wires and tubes that were connected to multiple machines.

Within a couple of hours we were ushered to a waiting room for family of intensive care patients. A uniformed policeman

spoke to us. He asked if we had any other children. At this point, we realized we needed to make arrangements to get Alex, Anthony's seven-year-old sister, off the school bus. Linda called her mother and father to take care of Alex. In the meantime, the police officer contacted his station which alerted Blue Ash Elementary to what had happened so that Alex's teacher could tell her that Grandma would get her off the bus that afternoon.

Since Anthony's "event" was as yet unidentified, the policeman asked about his possible use of drugs and alcohol, no doubt something the authorities had to investigate. The officer told us they needed to search his locker. We were sure he had never done any kind of drugs; in fact he disliked the way even a cola made him feel. But since we had no idea what had happened, we welcomed any clue that might help the doctors improve his condition.

We were told that Anthony was in critical condition. He might not make it through the night. I was stunned. My brain couldn't assimilate this news. He was fine this morning when I left for my appointment. Was this really true? Could he really die? I vacillated between disbelief and outright terror. Nah. No way. He just overdid it this weekend and was having a reaction to all the activity. I knew my son much better than these strangers. He would be fine by tomorrow. He was tough. He would be up and around within a couple of days, reliving all the excitement.

The ICU nurses recommended that we bring Anthony familiar items, his own t-shirts that he could wear instead of hospital gowns, and things that would remind him of home. About six p.m., Linda ran home to see Alex and to grab some clothes for the three of us.

Whenever our kids were sick, they always wanted their

mom close by. And since Linda couldn't be with them every moment, they learned to make do with one of her feather pillows which they carried around day and night. Their own little piece of mom, it comforted them when she wasn't there. That night, Linda brought one of her pillows to Anthony, hoping that as his head lay on it, he would be comforted, knowing that she was nearby.

Around eight p.m., Rob Lantman, one of the EMTs who had been on the squad that afternoon, came by to see how Anthony was doing. About twenty years old and new on the job, Rob told us how this, his first emergency run, had been difficult given that the victim was a child in full cardiac arrest. He had been so affected that he had to see Anthony and speak with us.

We pieced the story together with his help and information from a conversation Linda had had with a friend of Anthony's who she had called when she had run home earlier. This is what we knew: *As Anthony was getting ready to play basketball after eating lunch, he turned to Dustin and said, "I don't have a pulse," then fell face first to the ground. Once the other kids recognized that he wasn't kidding, they called the playground monitor who summoned other staff, including the school nurse. Seeing blood they were afraid to move him, afraid they might risk injuring his neck or back. Realizing that he was unconscious and not breathing they rolled him over to give him mouth-to-mouth resuscitation. In the meantime emergency ambulance crews from Blue Ash and Montgomery were called.*

Montgomery Fire and Rescue arrived first. Rob told us that Anthony was the color of faded blue jeans when he first caught sight of him. The EMTs sliced away his clothes, his bloody t-shirt, shorts and underwear. Once they cut away his clothes, they were able to work on resuscitating him without interference. His airway was

blocked, so they searched for and removed an obstruction and inserted a breathing tube. Normal color began to come back to Anthony. The paramedics shocked his heart with a defibrillator numerous times as they tried to stabilize him, but couldn't produce a normal rhythm. They then injected sodium bicarbonate into his bloodstream.

Anthony was airlifted from the playground. In route, EMTs used the defibrillator thirteen more times. Anthony's heartbeat was dangerously rapid and erratic as the helicopter flew to Children's Hospital Emergency Room.

Rob promised to stay in touch. Shortly after he left, Norm Barnhart showed up. Anthony had played baseball and basketball on the same teams as Norm's son, John David. We had gotten to know each other well over the years, attending games, organizing end-of-season parties and carpooling together. Norm had been in Columbus on business when his wife, Sally, called to tell him that Anthony had been airlifted to Children's. Instead of going home, he drove straight to the hospital from Columbus.

Norm was a great guy, warm and friendly and with a slight southern drawl, having grown up in Lexington, Kentucky. When you talked with Norm, you knew that he wasn't thinking about anything other than that particular conversation and that moment in time. He was genuinely interested in you and what you had to say. Easy going and affable, Norm was everybody's friend.

I was surprised to see him, not realizing that word had gone around about Anthony's emergency. Linda and I had been watching over Anthony, looking for any sign of change when Norm appeared outside the glass wall. No doubt he had taken in the scene and understood that there was no positive change

and things were certainly worse than he had hoped. After all, who could ever envision the Bernstein Black Sox starting first baseman in a coma?

I left the room to talk with Norm. He put his hands on my shoulders, looked me in the eyes and pulled me to him before he even said a word.

"What in the world happened?" Norm asked in his soft southern drawl.

"All we know is that he passed out on the playground. His heart stopped. But we don't know why. He has never had any problems like this. We just don't know anything yet."

Norm stayed for an hour or so and left, undoubtedly happy to go home to his healthy family, relieved that it wasn't John David, or his youngest son, Thomas, lying in a bed at Children's.

At about 10 p.m., as we kept vigil, Anthony's heart rate began to climb. The monitor had displayed a relatively consistent 135–155 beats per minute. But the numbers rocketed to 160, then 170, then 180, and soon reached over 200 beats per minute. This had to be bad—and dangerous. Staffers rushed into the room and went to work in an urgent flurry of activity.

Looking in from outside Anthony's room we could see the heart monitor's ever-increasing numbers—210, 230, 250 up to 280 beats per minute. We were frightened as the staff frantically searched for and located the EKG equipment, eventually placing the leads on his chest after some discussion.

By that time, Anthony's heart rate was well above 280 and they couldn't stabilize him. Nurses hurried in and out of the room, assuring us they were doing the best they could, that the doctors would give him a drug to slow his heart rate. In the meantime, we stood by helplessly, wondering what Anthony

was feeling, wondering if he was aware enough to know what was going on, wondering if he would die. Eventually they stabilized his heart, emergency staff dispersed and Anthony was quiet once again.

I wandered down the hall, needing time to recover from this terrifying episode. I entered a small waiting area that Children's Hospital provides just for families, affording parents an escape from the overwhelming tension that permeates a critically ill child's room. The reception area was empty and quiet, the TV tuned to the ten o'clock news. I found a secretarial chair, part of a desk setting with a telephone and phone directories. This mini office enabled parents access to the outside world so that they could conduct any necessary business of their lives while being held captive in the ICU, a place that seemed like another planet to those of us who didn't live in the world of health care.

I looked around the room, glad that all of the upholstered chairs were empty and I was alone. Straddling the seat, I draped my arms over the backrest, lay my head on them and closed my eyes. My thoughts were all over the place searching for reassurance that Anthony would be all right. I remembered back to when I played football, how I would come off the field while losing at halftime and I'd persuade myself to play harder and smarter when we took the field again. I would convince myself that we would win the game.

This time, the situation was out of my hands and my ability to change the outcome was greatly limited, nearly nonexistent. My contribution would have to come from the sidelines as an observer. I had to rely on God and his plans for Anthony and for our family. I knew that God was the dominant player in this scenario. I knew that He would help me deal with whatever happened. I began to talk to Him. I don't remember

exactly what I said. I do remember that I never asked "Why?" There often wasn't an answer to this question. I knew that life events happened and my approach had always been "Okay, how can I make the best out of this?"

Eventually, God spoke to me, "Anthony is going to make it. But there will be a price."

"That's it? Nothing else?" But no explanation was forthcoming. God had assured me that Anthony would live and that was all. I knew I had to have faith that God would look over us. I had to take comfort in His few words. But, what did He mean, there will be a price?

I should have been thrilled to know that Anthony would live. In fact, I was relieved, but for a split second I had a feeling that there might be more to this message. I dismissed it as I headed back to the ICU.

A great weight had been lifted from me and I was able to breathe easier as I entered Anthony's room where Linda was standing vigil, talking in low tones to the night nurse. We stayed with Anthony until early morning, sleeping for a few hours in one of the rooms the hospital provides for the parents of children in crisis.

CHAPTER 3

Day Two

SEPTEMBER 9, 1998

I woke to the sounds of Linda getting dressed in the dark.

"What time is it?" I asked.

"I'm not sure," she said.

We didn't have the advantage of checking our cell phones for the time as signs throughout the hospital reminded everyone to turn them off.

Our sleeping room was just big enough to hold two single beds and a small chest. It was situated in the middle of the sixth floor of the Children's Hospital tower so there were no windows that might allow us to see a lightening sky, which might give a clue as to the time of day. We dressed and hurried to the ICU to see Anthony, both of us confident that he would be sitting up in bed looking for a breakfast of chocolate milk, pancakes and eggs, his favorite meal morning or night.

As we entered the unit, we peered through the glass and saw Anthony lying motionless. There had been no change in his condition. He laid there still, the busy noise of the ICU all around him.

While Anthony had never been outgoing, he had always loved to tell stories about his sports activities, usually about a specific play or a shot on the basketball court. If he had been able, he would have waved us in and told us all about his last eighteen hours in elaborate detail. Instead, he lay on his back, his arms at his sides, resting on top of the sheet that covered him to his chest. Above the sheet, his face showed the trauma of his playground fall. His left cheek was still an open wound, his left eye swollen nearly shut.

Machines monitored his body temperature, blood pressure, heart, respiration, and oxygen saturation rates. Monitors in his room recorded these vital statistics and sent them to the central nursing station. He was hooked up to an IV and several other wires and tubes. A catheter directed his urine to a bag that hung on the side of the bed. The whirr of the feeding pump and the beeping of the heart monitor gave an eerie quality to the otherwise silent room of our twelve-year-old child.

As we watched our comatose son, an attending nurse administered medication through the IV in Anthony's right arm.

"Have there been any changes?" Linda asked as she stood next to the bed, holding Anthony's hand in hers.

The nurse turned to look at her and said, "His vitals have been steady for several hours now and he made it through the night. Honey, this is a good sign."

This was true, particularly to a nurse who works in ICU and cares for children who die. But this news was far less optimistic than that we had hoped to hear.

"When will the doctors be here?" I asked. We had learned that they travelled in a pack, at least in ICU. The nurse was noncommittal, saying only that they would be there sometime

that morning, probably between eight and eleven a.m. It was about six thirty so we decided to go to the cafeteria for coffee and breakfast in order to be back to talk with the doctors when they made their rounds.

We rode the elevator to the main floor of the hospital and made our way down the wide hall to the cafeteria. As we walked, we talked about how Anthony might fall behind in his school work and wondered how many days he might miss.

"I need to get his school assignments so he can get back to work as soon as he comes to. The good news is that school just started and the teachers are reviewing last year's material, so he's not missing a lot of new stuff," Linda said.

I agreed with Linda. While Anthony's grades were mostly Bs, we had to push him to do his homework. He liked school well enough, but mostly for the opportunity to socialize and play basketball at recess.

Anthony had been excited about entering the seventh grade because of the freedom, different campus and social events that junior high school meant. Just the week before, he and Linda had found his locker and planned out the route to his classes which were located in several different buildings on the grounds. We discussed how this recent event might interfere with him attending his first homecoming game and dance, events that he had been eagerly anticipating.

"I hope he will be back to school before homecoming. He is already talking about the game and the dance," Linda said.

"I can't imagine that he wouldn't be. It's almost a month away," I said.

We planned to go to the game too. We thought it would be fun to participate in this fall custom. Besides, while Anthony may have been ready to leave his mom behind, Linda wasn't

quite ready for her twelve year old to be left to his own devices. She had also signed up to chaperone the dance.

The cafeteria was calm, being relatively early for visitors. Mostly staff, dressed in green scrubs or nurses' uniforms sporting Winnie the Pooh and Scooby Doo patterns, occupied the tables. Linda filled Styrofoam cups with coffee from one of the large stainless steel urns, while I spooned scrambled eggs and sausage onto a plate. I paid the cashier and we found a table.

As we sat down, the glint of the acutely angled morning sun cast a glow in the room. I was momentarily dazed. How could the sun rise, like it did every morning, as though nothing at all had happened? As though all was well and my son wasn't in intensive care. Unconsciously, I had anticipated that this particular Wednesday would be grey and cloudy, respectful that something terrible had transpired.

We waited impatiently for the doctors. Around nine o'clock they came by Anthony's room. In a brief meeting next to his bed, they told us what they knew at this early stage.

They were able to get an EKG the night before when Anthony's heart rate spiked. The resident cardiologist recognized a pattern that identified the underlying cause of his cardiac arrest as Wolf Parkinson White (WPW) syndrome. He explained that Anthony's heart had an extra abnormal electrical pathway that allowed opposing electrical currents to collide, causing the cardiac arrest and turning this crucial organ into a "mass of quivering jelly."

The extra pathway would have to be ablated—cauterized—to seal it off so that there would be no future events. But, the cardiologist said, it would be awhile before Anthony's condition would be stable enough to perform this procedure. In the

meantime, his heart would be closely monitored. While Linda's mom had had a mild heart attack many years ago, she had recuperated and hadn't experienced any other problems. Since neither my family nor Linda's had any other history of heart disease, we were shocked. Anthony had always been a healthy kid, strong and athletic. He had never complained of anything more than a sore throat and the usual childhood illnesses. In fact, he had had a physical exam for athletics the week before which had revealed nothing unusual.

Apparently WPW isn't necessarily genetic and is only present in about two percent of the population. In many cases, people with WPW experience episodes of elevated heart rate that indicate an abnormal symptom which would be cause for alarm. Unfortunately, Anthony either never experienced symptoms, or perhaps having lived with them from birth, never thought to complain of them.

The cardiologist ordered EKGs for our immediate family, including my daughter, Ashley, who lived with her mom in northern Kentucky. He wanted to rule out the possibility of a familial WPW disorder. Recently, a teenage girl had experienced a severe cardiac event similar to Anthony's. While she was at Children's, the cardiologist discovered that her father and a sister shared the disorder. Because of the doctor's diligence, the family was saved from future surprise events. Obviously, they hoped to do the same for us.

We had a brief scare when Ashley's EKG came back indicating abnormalities. A second test was performed immediately and this one came back clean. Anthony was the only one of us with any type of electrical heart defect.

I called my clients to let them know what had happened, that Linda and I were both out of the office, and were currently

at the hospital night and day. I would stay in touch and be back to work shortly.

I called Tim Murray, the CEO at USI New England, to tell him what had happened, saying that I might have to cancel a training session scheduled for next week. Tim and I had gotten to be good friends over the last several months, and when I told him that Anthony had had a heart attack and was in a coma, he was distressed. He and his wife, Eileen, had three children of their own. Shortly after I met him he had missed one of my visits because his daughter, Sara, was hospitalized with a broken back due to a snowboarding accident. Tim knew all too well the pain and fear that a child with a severe injury evokes.

"Tony, forget about the training. Take care of Anthony and the family. We will continue to pay you. We'll catch up later," Tim assured me.

"Thanks, Tim. I'm sure Anthony will be fine. It's just a matter of time," I said.

"Eileen and I will pray for Anthony." I could hear the concern in Tim's voice. I promised to keep him posted.

As I got off the phone, I wondered where everything went so wrong. Just yesterday morning, Anthony called up the stairs that he was leaving to catch the school bus. I had been getting ready to go to a morning meeting with a potential prospect. Did I miss something? He seemed fine.

CHAPTER 4

The Initial Consultation

SEPTEMBER 11, 1998

The next several days were all about waiting for something to happen. We waited for Anthony to show signs that he was awakening. We waited for the doctors to tell us something new. We waited for Anthony's condition to stabilize so that he could tolerate the recommended MRI and CT scans that might tell us more about his condition. Anthony remained unresponsive. Nurses were in and out of his room, performing medical regimens—administering drugs, emptying and measuring urine output, writing numbers in charts, adding solution to the I.V. bag or adjusting settings on one machine or another.

When one is in a coma, the lungs build up fluids from lack of use, which can cause pneumonia. And so three or four times a day, a respiratory therapist would roll Anthony to one side. With hands cupped, she would pound his back to loosen the fluids that might have accumulated.

On Thursday, Anthony began to have seizures for long periods of time. These were painful to watch, as he would moan and shake. His back arched and his sweaty face contorted, as he

spasmed in the throes of torment. Medical personnel called these episodes "neurological storms." Over time, they became more frequent until eventually he seemed to be storming all the time. Sedation provided temporary relief, but within two to three hours, the convulsions would start all over again.

A physician regularly opened Anthony's eyelids to shine a pen light on his pupils to check dilation, tickled his toes to see if he pulled his foot away, or stimulated the palm of his hand in the hopes that he would close his fingers.

Several times a day a doctor asked Anthony to touch his nose. He didn't lift an arm or move at all. Could he even hear? The doctors told us that his prognosis became less optimistic the longer he remained unresponsive.

Finally, Anthony was stable enough to tolerate an MRI. We were elated when one of the doctors gave us good news. "Anthony has no swelling in his brain. He won't need a stent. It looks like he will be OK."

Word spread in our community that Anthony was at Children's Hospital and, by Thursday, a number of people, mostly men, came to visit. Some were clients I had grown close to and some were parents and coaches that I had worked with as president of the Sycamore Athletic Club, the local youth league. I think the men came because they, too, had sons and could relate to the fear that I might lose Anthony. I think the women, the mothers, couldn't bear to witness a child they knew in such dire physical condition; the reality of what had happened to Anthony was too much for them to assimilate, so most stayed away. But the husbands and fathers came to the hospital and stood outside of his room with me.

I imagine that most Intensive Care Units aren't particularly fond of having people milling about. ICUs aren't set up to

accommodate a lot of visitors, probably because personnel need to work quickly and people present distraction and obstruction that could interfere with emergency operations. But Children's had a different perspective on this, perhaps recognizing that a child in distress touches many lives on multiple levels or maybe knowing that the parents need particular attention that the hospital isn't able to deliver.

In the time that Anthony was in ICU, those who came to support us were never once asked to leave and, in fact, at one point a nurse commented on having never seen "so many tall men in ICU before." It seemed there were often seven to eight men standing vigil outside of Anthony's glass room. Or, maybe they were watching over Linda and me, recognizing how they would feel in similar circumstances. Like us, they stood around because there was nothing any of us could do. We talked idly, filling up empty space and time, and waited.

Some people come in and out of your life quickly, leaving you shaking your head and wondering what happened. Steve Blieden was one of those people. He always left an impression, sometimes a questionable one. He had two boys, one of whom played football with Anthony in Sycamore Athletic Club, and Steve and his wife would run concessions at the games and produce each season's program. About 5'10" dark haired, dark eyed, outspoken and assertive, Steve alienated as many people as he befriended. But, those of us running SAC loved working with him because we knew he would get the job done, whichever job he was assigned.

Steve showed up at the hospital within the first several days of Anthony's tragedy. He didn't know many of the other people standing outside of the glass walled room, so he stood alone, off to one side, watching. Linda and I had been talking with

one of the nurses, hoping to get an update on when a CT scan would be run, when we noticed him. The doctors had decided to postpone the scan until Anthony was in a more stable condition. We were frustrated at the lack of information after two days, but agreed that we didn't want to do anything that might worsen Anthony's situation. Disheartened, we made our way over to Steve and gave him an update. There had been no change, we told him. Anthony was still in a coma following his cardiac arrest on the playground.

Steve surprised Linda and me by saying something that seemed totally out of character. "Use me like a piece of furniture," he said. "If you need to lean on me, I'm here. Otherwise, just ignore me." His offer was moving. We had never seen this side of Steve.

He came to the hospital many times in the coming days. We would see him standing in his usual spot, at the outside corner of Anthony's room. One day Linda and I were voicing our dissatisfaction about a promised consultation by the head neurologist that we couldn't seem to get scheduled. Such delays were not unusual in the world of medicine, but we were desperate to get some answers and had been nagging the nurses to get this conference scheduled.

Steve must have overheard and taken our concerns to heart, because later that day he introduced us to the head neurologist. While we had been "ignoring" him, per his initial advice, he had searched, located and coerced the doctor into accompanying him to Anthony's room. We scheduled a conference for the next day.

Linda, her younger sister Jeni, and I sat in the conference room with pens, notebooks and questions. Several doctors were present, including Children's head neurologist, a cardiologist, a

physiatrist, otherwise known as a rehabilitation doctor, and a clutch of resident interns.

The head neurologist started. "Your son suffers from global anoxic brain injury. This happened when his brain was deprived of oxygen for seven to ten minutes during his cardiac arrest and resuscitation."

We were thinking he was in a coma because he hit his head on the pavement when he lost consciousness. We had been told by one of the residents that there was no swelling of the brain, and that Anthony's prognosis was good. We were sure that any moment now, he would come out of his coma and be fine. This was not what we were expecting.

"Will he be okay?"

"At this point it appears that he will not die."

"What does that mean? When will he come out of the coma?"

"We don't know when. It may be several days or weeks. He may remain unresponsive."

"How long will he be in the hospital? Will he be going back to school soon?" We were still certain that he would be fine, that he would come back to us.

"We don't know how long he will be here."

"Will he be normal?"

"He has a twenty percent chance of being independent."

"What does that mean?"

"It means that there is a twenty percent chance that he will be able to lead an independent lifestyle."

"What is an independent lifestyle?"

"It means that he would have the ability to take care of himself."

"Hell, Anthony is only a kid. I know adults who aren't

independent," I said. "He moves his toes when the doctors touch them. Doesn't that mean something?"

"This is a reflex. It doesn't require conscious use of the brain. It is only significant in that it tells us that there are brainwaves present."

"Will he ever walk again?"

"It is unlikely."

"If you don't believe he will walk again, I want a new doctor," I demanded. "One who believes that Anthony will fully recover. Your attitude will not contribute to his recovery."

"We understand, Mr. Cole."

"When can we start therapy?" I was convinced that he would be fine, that he would walk, that I would help him walk again.

"Once his heart is ablated and he has been moved into Rehabilitation."

"When will that be?"

"We don't know. He must be able to tolerate the operation. His condition is still unstable. It could be several weeks before he is strong enough. He will be moved shortly to the Continuing Care Unit, where he will stay until he is stable enough to go to Cardiac Care. After his heart is ablated he will transfer to Rehabilitation."

"What are you doing to help him? All I see are people coming and going, giving him drugs, opening his eyelids, asking him to touch his nose. Shouldn't you be doing something else?"

"We are doing everything we can."

"Well, clearly that's not good enough. What you're doing isn't working. So you need to do something else. What are other hospitals doing for cases like this?"

"Mr. Cole, we are doing everything we can."

CHAPTER 5

Coaching Young Anthony

EARLY MARCH 1998

I'm coaching basketball for Anthony and his buddies in one of the last games of the '97–98 season in Blue Ash, Ohio. I never had better than a .500 season with his basketball teams. My prior coaching experience translated into success on the baseball diamond and on the football field, but his basketball teams suffered a bit. Not the kids' fault. It just wasn't my best game.

We're at the Greene Intermediate School and the gymnasium is crowded. Anthony has been doing a hero's job all afternoon trying to defend a skinny kid that must be three inches taller than he is. My yelling isn't helping much, but Anthony is hanging tough.

One of his favorite NBA players, someone we watch all the time together in the den-of-sports-fans, is Dikembe Mutombo, now a free agent pickup with the Atlanta Hawks. At 7'2", Mutombo is one of the famous "big men" in the league and a huge defensive presence. What Anthony seems to love, almost as much as Mutombo's skill, is his personality, his on-court charisma. It's usually the 3-point-shooting offensive players that appeal to 12-year-olds, but not my boy. He loves this strange, Congolese giant with huge hands.

When Mutombo blocks a shot, his signature defensive stuff, he wags a long index finger at the recently humbled offensive player, and silently says, "Oh, no you don't, my friend." The TV cameras love it. So does Anthony.

This skinny, taller kid that Anthony has struggled with all afternoon has been getting more confident as the game wears on. I don't want to call Anthony over and warn him about it openly—nothing can demoralize your own team as much as the coach's kid being brought over to the sidelines for a private chat with the coach/dad. It's just not done, if you can help it—so I keep my mouth shut and watch them battle back and forth on the court. I can feel a shot coming from this kid, though, and I hope my boy is braced for it.

I freeze on the sideline as time slows. This kid is breaking down the court and Anthony is just a step in front of him. My fists clench. I know what's coming. But then the kid holds up a half-hitch for some reason and Anthony is three steps down the court now, planting and turning like I've taught him, and poised. The skinny kid goes for it, takes the shot. But Anthony's right hand is up, above the ball, and it's a clean, beautiful stuff! The skinny kid's wrist bends helplessly back as the ball heads out of bounds and the shot is dead.

Anthony lands cleanly, turns to me and in slow motion, wags the Mutombo finger. I'm laughing now, as proud as I've ever been in my life, wondrous at the unspoken exchange that just took place between us and our evolving relationship.

CHAPTER 6

ICU to CCU to Cardiac Care

SEPTEMBER 12 TO OCTOBER 28, 1998

By day nine at Children's, Anthony was considered stable enough to move to the Continuing Care Unit of the hospital, which was on the same floor just down the hall from ICU. The area was identical to the one he had just left, with glass front rooms and a central nursing station, but the level of care required by these patients was less critical. However, since Anthony's condition hadn't changed appreciably and his heart was still not ablated, he required continual nursing supervision.

Flowers, cards, balloons and gift baskets were delivered regularly. The students from Anthony's math class made a get-well poster, which they all signed. The principal from Sycamore Junior High came to visit. The pastor of our church stopped to pray for us. Anthony's best friend, Nick, and his mom came by every few days to see him. His step-sister, Ashley, and her mom, Sue, came to visit. They took Alex to lunch, giving her some much needed personal attention.

Linda and I were still at the hospital during the day, but while she stayed with Anthony most nights, I went home to

take care of Alex so that Grandma and Grandpa could go home to rest. By this time, the sleeping rooms in the hospital were often needed by parents of patients in the ICU, so sometimes Linda would sleep on the window cushion in Anthony's room. Technically the hospital didn't permit parents to stay overnight in the room, but the nurses knew they would do the same under the circumstances and never told her to leave.

By day ten, Linda and I decided that it was time to get Anthony up, reasoning that the human body isn't built to lay flat perpetually. So when the physical therapist came to stretch Anthony's arms and legs, we requested that she help us get him into a wheelchair. This was an ordeal because he was still hooked up to monitors, an I.V., a feeding pump, and a catheter. Two nurses, the physical therapist and I each took a limb, lifted him and placed him in the wheelchair that sat alongside his bed, while Linda and another nurse guided the leads and tubes.

Anthony hadn't been upright in over a week and the therapist told us that he would have to get accustomed to sitting after lying supine for so long. He sat in the wheelchair in diapers, head lolling to one side, arms limp in his lap for only five minutes, the length of time the therapist recommended. The nurses monitored his vitals closely for the few minutes he sat. We then reversed the whole operation and put him back in bed.

Since he had tolerated sitting up, the therapist agreed to make this a daily event. We got Anthony up each day, increasing the length of time he sat in the wheelchair by a few minutes as time went on. I had become accustomed to seeing him lying in bed, but initially the sight of my son, drooling and propped up by pillows was a shock. I was stunned and embarrassed that he wasn't even able to control his saliva. But, I knew that getting him in an upright position was important to his recovery.

I resolved to get over my embarrassment and do whatever it took to help him recover.

The therapist taught us how to stretch Anthony's arms, legs, hands and feet to prevent his joints from becoming stiff and fixed. She would come by a couple times a day, pick up each limb and move it back and forth at the joint. She reminded us that his body would soon lose its ability to perform if it wasn't used. Her job was to keep Anthony's physical ability intact so that when he was able to move again, the joints and muscles would be functional. Jeni, Linda and I supplemented her visits, following her instructions.

Because Anthony's right knee and both elbows were beginning to contract, she ordered custom-made splints. These splints were made of fabric and heavy batting with Velcro straps to keep each joint straight. Since she had them custom sewn, she ordered them covered in a material with a sports print that was suitable for a twelve-year-old boy. He wore these splints for several hours a day.

She also created fiberglass splints for his ankles and feet to prevent foot drop, a condition that happens when the muscles in the calf shorten from lack of use, causing the toes to point downward so that the sole of the foot is no longer parallel to the ground. Permanent foot drop can make standing difficult because the solid base that is provided by the bottom of the foot is gone. Walking becomes arduous because the foot has to be raised further when taking a step so that the toes clear the ground. Our goal, per the physical therapist, was to keep Anthony's ankles flexible and his feet properly positioned, allowing him the ability to stand and walk again someday.

I wondered why this was so important since I was sure he was just a short time away from sitting up and saying, "Hi

Dad!" and telling me he was thirsty. Surely, he would be up and moving around soon, wondering when he could go back to school so he could tell his buddies about his helicopter ride, even if he had to make it up since he wouldn't remember the actual event. I was confident he would walk out of here in a few weeks.

On day fourteen, September 22, we heard that Anthony was stable enough to move to the Cardiac Care unit. We were very excited. This meant that he would soon have the ablation and we knew he would move from there to Rehab. On Wednesday, Anthony was moved, bed and all, through the halls and elevators to his new room.

As we settled Anthony into his new room, Timothy Knilans, the pediatric cardiologist who would perform the ablation, stopped by to visit. He examined Anthony and told us that it would be a couple of weeks before he would perform the operation. He was leaving for vacation and wouldn't schedule the surgery until after he returned. How frustrating! We had hoped that it would be done as soon as Anthony had arrived in the cardiac care unit.

Once again we were waiting for something to happen. A couple of weeks stretched to a month. Anthony had not gained consciousness. He seemed to be in a continual state of storming. We brought in a portable fan, which the hospital had to check and approve. We used the fan to help cool him because he sweated profusely while storming. We wiped his face, arms and chest with a cool, wet cloth every fifteen to thirty minutes. I was exhausted just watching him and wondered how his body could tolerate this nearly constant state of physical exertion akin to running back-to-back marathons at a sprinter's pace.

I went to the hospital less, taking care of Alex and turning

to my clients for distraction. There was nothing I could do at Children's and I was covering for both Linda and me at the office. I stayed busy creating new material and talking to clients who assured me that they would be fine until the situation allowed me to feel comfortable enough to leave home.

At night, after Alex was asleep, I would play the video games that Anthony and I had played together. As I manipulated the controls, I would think of the hours we had spent moving players of "NBA Live" around on the screen of the TV. I imagined that he was there with me, laughing at something one of my players did or commenting on a stupid move I made. I must remember to tell him about this play or that, I would think, knowing that he would get a kick out of some of my blunders.

I also began surfing the Internet to learn more about Anthony's condition and to search for any therapies or medicines that might better his prognosis. Most of the information was useful in helping me understand his anoxic brain injury, but it was also less than optimistic. I did find, however, that there was a clinic in Florida that was seeing amazing progress in certain patients with brain injury by using Hyperbaric Oxygen Therapy. HBOT, as it is otherwise known, was originally developed to help deep sea divers recover from decompression illness, the "bends," a condition resulting from ascending to the surface of the water too quickly. HBOT was also an approved therapy for carbon monoxide poisoning and for tissue breakdown, but not for brain injury.

The more I read, the more intrigued I became. The patient sits or lies in a sealed glass chamber into which pure oxygen is pumped. The chamber gradually increases the amount and pressure of oxygen, forcing the patient's body to absorb more than it would otherwise. According to his website, Dr. Richard

Neubauer was demonstrating successful recovery of some patients with brain injury at his clinic in Ft. Lauderdale using this therapy. I sent away for the video mentioned on his website.

After the second week of Anthony's stay in cardiac care, Linda began to come home frequently to sleep. At this point, Anthony was in a private room with an armchair that converted to a bed and while she could stay with him, Linda was finding it impossible to rest. She was exhausted. Recognizing that he would be in the hospital for awhile, she had to think long term. She needed to spend time with Alex and get some sleep.

On October 27, Dr. Knilans and the operating team spent seven hours ablating Anthony's heart while we sat in the waiting room. When he finally met with us he explained that the area requiring ablation was larger than expected. He had had to go back several times to seal off the extra pathway which extended the operating time by several hours. But Dr. Knilans felt sure he had repaired the problem area within his heart and Anthony had tolerated the procedure well.

Anthony was monitored closely for another twenty four hours within the cardiac care unit. Once the monitor records verified that the defect had been corrected, we were notified he would be transferred to Rehabilitation the next day. After more than a month of living in this particular room, we had accumulated lots of things. Linda and I packed up clothes, books, gifts, cards, splints, Anthony's radio/CD player that we had brought from home and the portable fan. We were anxious with anticipation having heard great things about Children's Rehab. Although he was still unconscious, we were sure that Anthony would improve by leaps and bounds once he was on a unit that focused on rehabilitation.

CHAPTER 7

Pig's Legs and Flapjacks

OCTOBER 29, 1998

We waited impatiently for the orderlies to come and take Anthony to Rehab, otherwise known as The Pavilion. The minutes turned into an hour and then to an hour and a half. I leaned over the bed to move Anthony from his back onto his side. We moved Anthony a lot, about every hour that we were there, to prevent him from getting bedsores. As I turned Anthony, I remembered:

We had just finished playing a football game against Clermont County Northeast. Anthony was playing for the eleven-year-old team, as a tight end, on offense. He had become a pretty good receiver and a better-than-average blocker. During the game he made a nice catch over the hands of a player on the opposing team, but took a hard hit to his rib cage as he reached up to make the catch. He managed to hold onto the ball, but hit the ground hard. After laying there recovering for a few minutes, he got up, shook his head to clear the cobwebs, and headed back to the huddle.

Later in the game the coach called the same play. Once again the quarterback threw the ball to Anthony. However, anticipating

another hit, Anthony 'short armed' the catch, instead of extending his arms fully to receive the ball, he kept them bent at the elbows, hoping to protect his rib cage. Also known as "alligator arms," this technique worked well to prevent injury, but hindered the receiver's ability to make the catch. Often the ball fell to the ground as an incomplete pass, as it did in this case.

On the drive home after the game, we stopped for a mint chocolate chip malt at United Dairy Farmers, our usual routine. After we'd placed our orders, we began to discuss the game and I congratulated Anthony on his great catch. "But what happened the second time the play was called?" I asked.

He looked at me sheepishly and said, "I got pig's legs."

"Pig's legs?"

"Yeah, you know, pig's legs."

"You mean alligator arms?"

He looked at me and suddenly it dawned on him what he had said. His eyes shone and he started to laugh. He shook his head and said, "Oh, man, I mean alligator arms. I got alligator arms." Then, in almost the same breath he asked, "Did you see my flapjack?"

Around the time of Anthony's heart attack there was an offensive tackle that played for the Ohio State University football team by the name of Orlando Pace. A great big mountain of a man, Orlando's signature was his ability to flatten an opposing blocker. This event became known, in the world of football, as a 'pancake.'

"Your flapjack?" I asked.

"Yeah, in the third quarter, Coach called a sweep with the tailback to my right. I got great position on the defensive end and I did a flapjack."

"A flapjack? You mean a pancake?"

The 'I can't believe I did it again' recognition, the smile in his eyes and the grin on his face gave way to "I mean pancake, the pancake, did you see it?"

"Yes, son. I did."

As I reached under his back to roll him onto his side, I was close enough to talk into his ear. I told the story to him and whispered, "Do you remember that day Anthony? Do you remember pig's legs and flapjacks?"

He opened his eyes and the slightest smile appeared on his face. I could have crumbled right there on the floor. Linda stared disbelieving, frozen at the foot of the bed. I kept talking about flapjacks and pig's legs. With every repeat of the words and the story, Anthony's eyes opened just a bit wider, and the small but visible smile grew. For the first time, there was recognition in his face. He was there somewhere. Thank God, my son was in there somewhere.

Damn, where was the camera? Linda found it after rifling through a couple of boxes and quickly snapped a picture in which my grinning face lay next to Anthony's, whose half open eyes and sleepy smile told us to have faith.

We were filled with hope and anticipation of full recovery as we followed the orderly through the halls to The Pavilion.

CHAPTER 8

Some Good Advice

OCTOBER 31, 1998

It was Halloween night, about seven weeks after Anthony went into the hospital. This was a tough night for us because, like all kids, Anthony loved trick or treating. The combination of dressing up and the prospect of all that free candy excited him. No doubt, Halloween presented a wonderful combination of fantasy and sugar that most kids loved. Anthony was no different, planning for this holiday a year in advance and announcing his chosen costume for next year only days after each Halloween. Like most kids, he changed his mind a few times throughout the year, after seeing some new character. He left no doubt that he was thinking hard about his presentation on this big evening.

As a young kid he was always pretending to be Batman, Superman, Michelangelo, one of the Ninja Turtles, or a Power Ranger, and had worn these costumes and a few more for Halloween before he had grown out of his superhero phase. In fact, for years Linda's mom kept a kitchen towel and a clothespin ready for his superhero fantasies. Whenever he was at Grandma

and Grandpa's house, he had a makeshift cape that instantly transformed him into whichever superhero he wished to be at that moment. Looking back, it seemed that he wore this cape and swooped around the house for eons, jumping off the sofa to tackle and wrestle an invisible villain to the ground, etching this memory in my mind forever.

But this year was different. This year he was in a coma. This year there was no superhero or pirate.

By the age of twelve, Anthony had grown out of his fascination with dressing up. The year before, we had constructed our own, rowdy version of this holiday that included a full-size standup of Elvis and karaoke in the front yard with our next door neighbors, the Ludys. No doubt, Anthony had anticipated this night, but for different reasons. He had developed a major crush on Michelle, Mike and Linda's beautiful daughter, and had looked forward to the opportunity to hang out with her. Michelle was a talented musician, playing the piano and singing with amazing skill for a twelve-year-old. She had sung karaoke with us the year before.

But our Halloween would look very different this year. There would be no karaoke or Elvis. This year Anthony didn't even know it was Halloween and was not allowed to leave the hospital. Linda's sister stayed with him that evening so that we could be with Alex, allowing her some normalcy on this important childhood holiday. This year, unlike past years, Alex's costume was a hasty, last minute, makeshift affair, that of a 60's era hippie, acceptable under the circumstances, but certainly not what she would have chosen. Looking back at the photos of that night, I recognize that her costume was indicative of the turmoil we were in, that her unkempt hair and sloppy clothes were reflective of Linda's and my preoccupation with Anthony.

Natalie, the Ludy's youngest daughter, was a year older than Alex and they had been best friends since we had moved into our house on what I liked to call "Mount Blue Ash." Our neighborhood was the highest point in the area; you had to climb a major hill off of Cooper or Hunt roads and wind around for a half-mile before arriving at the top, where we lived.

This Halloween, Natalie was also dressed as a hippie and both girls were anticipating how many houses they could hit and how much candy they could amass in the time that Mike and I would accompany them.

Linda had picked up a pizza on her way home from the hospital and had coerced Alex into sitting and eating a slice, but when Natalie arrived, they were both impatient to get started. After all, it was 6:05 p.m. and Trick-or-Treat had begun five minutes ago. They were losing valuable time.

Often Halloween night is accompanied by a cold snap, and this was one of those years when all the perfectly planned costumes would be covered by winter coats. The girls donned their winter coats, covering their hippie outfits, and picked up their pillowcases, obviously expecting a big haul of candy. Then they led me and Mike into the cold evening air.

Both Lindas stayed behind to dole out candy while Mike and I headed out the door, following Natalie, who always wanted to run, never walk, to where she was headed. Mike and I started down the dark street, hearing little voices around us before we were actually able to see the forms of other trick-or-treaters and the parents who accompanied them. Natalie had planned the route, so we followed as she and Alex led us out of the cul-de-sac and to points farthest from our home. On the way, the girls ran through each of the well kept yards to the front door, rang the bell, did the necessary greeting,

collected their treats and hurried to the next house. Mike and I heard the girls' excited voices comparing and commenting on each deposit made into their bags as they ran from house to house.

Mike and I talked as we walked. We had become good friends since we had moved into the neighborhood. We were both about the same age, both businessmen, and we had a fair amount in common, including yards in which moles were persistent pests. We were forever trying to catch and dispose of these tunneling animals as they made small cities just below the ground, judging by the network of linear disruptions in the mulch and grass. What had started as a serious venture of ridding our yards of these destructive creatures turned into an obviously unsuccessful, but comical routine as Mike or I would find a sprung trap and announce a capture. At this point, all at-home family members would gather around to sing "I'm the Mole Man" to the tune of "Soul Man," emulating John Belushi of the Blues Brothers. We all enjoyed the ritual mostly because it gave us the chance to laugh. Clearly the moles were winning this ground war.

Unless I'm training professionally, I don't usually do much of the talking in a conversation, opting instead to ask questions and listen. But when Mike asked how Anthony was doing, I unloaded everything I'd been keeping in. "Anthony isn't doing anything. He's in bed most of the day and all night. He is sedated all the time because otherwise he has what they call "neurological storms," Now that he is on the Rehab floor, he has physical, occupational and speech therapy sessions twice a day but he's unable to do anything they ask."

I continued to voice my impatience and aggravation. "I always thought that he would wake up and be fine. But he hasn't

and the doctors tell us that the longer he is in a coma, the worse the prognosis."

We had been walking for almost an hour when the girls ran over chattering about their more exciting treats and asking if they could keep going. Usually, I am impatient and am ready to be home after an hour of trick or treating, but this night there was only the empty bedroom of my son to remind me of how much I missed him after seven weeks. Having nowhere to go but home, every square foot of which reminded me of Anthony, and having no way to escape, I welcomed any form of distraction.

Mike picked up the conversation where I left off. "When Chris was diagnosed with cancer I nearly lost my mind with worry. My God, he was only nine years old and I thought he might die. I spent every waking moment with him or talking with doctors or researching treatments.

"In retrospect, I have some regrets. I took my eye off our business, thinking it would still be there when we got through our nightmare. But by the time I could focus on business again, my major client had replaced me and I didn't have any new business coming in. By the end of the year I was looking for a job."

"I hope you don't make the mistake I made when I stopped paying attention to the business. It might not be there when you're ready to come back to it."

I absently acknowledged Mike's words, recognizing as I did, that I had no intention of neglecting Anthony Cole Training Group and, being the driven personality I am, I was itching to get back to work and to my clients. Mike's advice did, however, reinforce the commitment I had to keeping our business on the right track just to be able to afford the hefty expenses that I knew would come our way.

By then I heard Alex telling Natalie that she was tired and wanted to go home. I knew she was also looking forward to spending some time with her mom who was waiting for her, knowing that she would have Linda's undivided and sorely missed attention for an hour or two until it was time to go to bed. Natalie, who always had more energy than any kid I knew, wanted to continue trick-or-treating, so Mike and Natalie continued on their Halloween pilgrimage.

I took Alex's hand in mine, needing a physical connection with my youngest child. Holding hands we headed home on this coldest and darkest of October nights.

CHAPTER 9

Thanksgiving

NOVEMBER 26, 1998

Anthony had been on the Pavilion for nearly a month. He was on the fourth floor, in a large private room with a window that looked out the front of the hospital. Had he been able to focus, he would have seen cranes constructing the new wing. But while he was physically present, his mind and spirit were absent and his body seemed more a container for live organs than a conscious being. We had thought, after his reaction to the pig's legs story, that he would begin to come out of his coma, but we had seen no signs of recovery since then.

By this time the wound on his face, caused from his fall to the playground, had healed. He had lost weight and was thinner. His face had taken on a vacant, distressed appearance, as though he was always frowning. His eyes were often open, but blank and unknowing. They now had an eerie quality about them, the pupils having dilated, causing his eyes to look inky black. When he wasn't storming, he lay unmoving and rigid in the hospital bed, head locked to one side, an effect of the neurological assault on his brain.

We had developed a pattern by this time. Typically Linda would go to the hospital after Alex left for school. She stayed until three or four o'clock every day, learning every aspect of Anthony's care. She learned about the feeding pump and medications, how to bathe Anthony in bed, how to transfer him into and out of bed. She accompanied him to procedures and tests. She was present at all therapy sessions and learned what the speech, occupational and physical therapists were doing with him and why. She knew the staff on the rehab floor well.

Linda's sister, Jeni, or I would come in shortly after she left. One of us would stay with Anthony through the evening, keeping him company, making sure his pump didn't run out of formula, stretching his limbs and making sure the nurses performed his bowel program. Anthony was now able to be in a wheelchair for thirty minutes consecutively and each of us was determined to get him out of his room for a few minutes regularly. In the evening, we walked him through the halls and underground tunnels of the hospital when it was too cold or rainy outside. Otherwise, we pushed him up and down the streets of "Pill Hill," desperate to do anything that would allow us a change of scenery and an escape from the monotony and depression of his hospital room.

During our walks, I talked to Anthony. The topics of these one-sided conversations ranged from sports and business to the story of his heart attack. I told him how he flew over the city in a helicopter and landed on the roof of the hospital, something he would have been thrilled to have consciously experienced. I told him how he nearly died, how he had been shocked with the defibrillator thirteen times while in the air, how the paddles had left burn marks on his chest. I recounted the story of his second

near death episode in the hospital which helped the doctors diagnose the abnormality in his heart.

I told him every day and in nearly every conversation that he would come out of this, that he would be okay because he had the heart of a champion. The fact that he had survived cardiac arrest twice at his young age was evidence that he was tough and determined to fight. "We have to believe. We have to have faith. We can never give up. We have to pray daily and ask God to help you recover. Faith makes anything possible," I said. "We'll shoot hoops on the driveway and play 'NBA Live' again," I promised.

Rehabilitation continued. Twice a day each of the physical, occupational and speech therapists would come to Anthony's room to take him to his session. The doctors told us that, in a severe case of brain injury like Anthony's, maximum progress would be made within the first eighteen to twenty-four months of the event and it was obvious that Children's staff was working hard to maximize this opportunity. It seemed that Anthony would barely get in bed for a rest before the next therapist showed up to work with him.

Linda, Jeni and I were committed to helping him get the most out of this eighteen to twenty four months, and so we each manipulated his arms, legs, hands, feet, fingers and toes, to prevent them from becoming fixed and spastic. We spent hours doing coma stimulation—exposing Anthony to different scents, textures, and noises with items that the therapists left behind. We talked to him, asked him to touch his nose or push a button, hoping to improve his almost nonexistent ability to perform when a therapist or doctor requested the same. We emulated the speech therapist, feeding him tiny tastes of sherbet that forced him to manipulate his lips, tongue and mouth in order to

manage the resulting saliva. Over time, the therapists recognized our dedication to rehabilitating Anthony and left us equipment to use over the weekend when they weren't working.

Each weekday the physical therapist would get him up on a tilt table. A big contraption, Anthony would be transferred onto a three by six foot wood platform while it was in horizontal position, so that the soles of his feet rested on the wood ledge at one end. Once strapped into place, using a remote control that operated the motor underneath the platform, the therapist would begin to tilt the board slowly, stopping at several intervals so that Anthony could adapt to the resulting change in equilibrium. Eventually, he would be upright and bearing weight for ten to twenty minutes before she reversed the process. While he was upright she would encourage him to reach for an item she would hold out to him. On the weekends the therapist would leave the tilt table for us and Linda and I would get him up each day, continuing her efforts.

Time dragged on while Anthony remained disconnected from the world around him. It seemed that overnight he began to grow hair in his pelvic region and on his chin. Oddly, his body seemed to go through puberty within a few days. He also developed a bald patch on the back of his head. The doctors told us that his brain injury was a probable catalyst for both phenomena.

Unfortunately, while staying in the cardiac care unit one night, Linda had seen a TV special that featured several severe traumatic brain injuries in which the afflicted individuals lay in bed, moaning and lost to our world, disfigured, nothing more than bedded vegetables. This special haunted her and she was convinced that if we talked to, touched and constantly stimulated Anthony in one form or another, we could keep him from

receding so far into the vast wasteland of coma, that he might not find his way back to us. So, on my evenings with him, I stretched his arms and legs and talked to him or read the sports section of the paper to update him on his favorite teams, particularly the Chicago Bulls. Occasionally, with the help of a nurse, I would put him in the bathtub. But there were many times when my efforts to engage him seemed futile. He gave no indication that he was present or benefitting at all. Sometimes, I resorted to turning on the TV to keep him company while I worked on my laptop, offering us a break from the pressure that continued to mount as time went on and he remained unresponsive.

Each night before I left, I would try to make him comfortable. The muscles of his neck were taut and so I would cradle his head in my hands and massage his skull while I gently rocked it back and forth. I would massage his neck while I told him how much I loved him. The combination of rocking motion and massage seemed to help him relax and sometimes he would even fall asleep. I would make sure his radio was tuned to B105, his favorite country station so that he could hear the music he loved. I would leave the hospital and walk to the parking lot, relieved to be out of this sad and depressing place, but despondent that he couldn't go home with me. It was unnatural to leave him, my child of twelve, behind. He had been to camp only once and not being one who wanted to be away from home, he had opted never to go again. I was sure, at some level, he missed being with us.

On my way home I would pass the UDF where he and I had stopped regularly for malts, a ritual we indulged in after each of his games. The familiar pink and black logo of the neon sign shone through the night, reminding me of the times we

had gone into the store, stood side by side and ordered our particular concoctions while dissecting this play or that.

I found myself avoiding situations that might trigger memories or where I might run into someone who would ask about him. Recently, I had experienced moments when I imagined I saw or heard him. Unexpectedly, a voice or a movement would catch my attention, and my heart would leap. A boy on a bike or a group of kids on a basketball court would catch me by surprise and suddenly tears would roll down my face.

There were times when I was sure that the loss of his presence was more than I could bear and I would think a six pack of beer might take me to another, happier place, at least for a little while. More than once, I drove up to the front of that lighted UDF store and parked, but I couldn't make myself go in.

It wasn't long before I found another convenience store, one that looked different, one that wouldn't remind me of mint chocolate malts and the many times I had taken Anthony for granted. But I never managed to buy anything more than milk or ice cream. There was nothing I could do, nowhere I could go, that would allow me to escape the loss of my son.

• • •

We had been preparing for weeks to take Anthony home for a few hours. Once the doctors and nurses were convinced that we were able to care for him properly, we were permitted to take him home from three until eight p.m. on Thanksgiving Day. We had written orders detailing his medical needs for the five hours he would be gone from the hospital. On Thanksgiving afternoon, Bob Scully, a friend and former co-worker of mine dropped by to visit. Bob helped us load Anthony into the

front seat with all his necessary diapers, splints, special cushions, medical supplies and a portable wheelchair into the trunk. As we drove home, Linda pointed out landmarks that Anthony would remember, including the junior high school stadium where we had kicked off the junior league season a couple months ago, and Crossgate Lanes, the bowling alley where we celebrated every New Year's Eve with his cousins, aunts and uncles. When we got to the house, I transferred him from the car into the wheelchair. Because of our frequent walks, I had become adept at navigating a wheelchair up and over curbs and easily pulled him up the front stoop and through the front entry. As we came into the house, Grandma, Grandpa, Jeni and Alex appeared, excited that Anthony was home after being gone for so long.

This was a big day for all of us. Each of us had missed him sorely over the ten weeks since his heart attack. To have Anthony with us again would lend some semblance of "family" to our Thanksgiving gathering. We were all looking forward to this day, knowing that his being home would fill the void that had recently consumed our lives.

I came around to the side of Anthony's chair as we stood in the foyer, encircled by his family. I scoured his face, hoping to see in his eyes, some recognition of his surroundings; looking for evidence that he was excited to be with the people he loved. Secretly, I had harbored hopes that being home would remind him of whom he had been before September 8 and that he would somehow be miraculously restored to his former self. But he sat unresponsive in his wheelchair, not recognizing that he was home with his family for the first time in almost three months.

The folding wheelchair didn't accommodate him very well,

although the therapists had found a cushion that supplemented the sling seat. When we walked him around "Pill Hill" we had to wrap a strap around his chest to keep him upright and wedge pillows between his side and the right arm of the wheelchair to keep his spastic body from leaning way out over the right side of the chair. We knew from experience that he couldn't tolerate sitting in the wheelchair for more than half an hour and since all the bedrooms were on the second floor, Linda and I transferred him into the taupe leather recliner in the family room that I had gotten for Father's Day last year.

Not long ago, this recliner had become his favorite seat in the house. We had only had it for a few months before he got sick, but I would often find him sitting in it when I came home. He would wrestle with me over who would have the privilege of occupying this sweet spot, knowing I would always, eventually win. But sometimes we would end up in it together, watching a game or a favorite movie.

It was wonderful having Anthony at home, even if he wasn't as he had been. There were jolting moments of stark reality when his ruined physical condition reminded me that he wasn't his former self, but we were all so relieved to have him back amongst us that we flocked around him, celebrating his return to our family center. Grandma had cooked a dinner of turkey and gravy, mashed potatoes and dressing and pumpkin pie for the holiday, but the meal was secondary to Anthony's first visit home. We each took turns sitting with him in the family room while the rest of us ate. We all wandered in and out of the family room, talking to Anthony, adjusting his pillows, holding his hand and visiting.

Soon it was seven thirty and time to leave. Linda and I transferred Anthony from the recliner to the wheelchair and

from wheelchair into the car, a time consuming process. We packed up his things and drove to the hospital. When we reached the rehab unit, the nurses greeted Anthony, asking how his visit home had been as they hooked up his feeding tube, changed his diaper and administered his medications. Linda puttered around, making excuses that she had to do this or that, delaying the time to leave. Eventually, he was settled in and we kissed Anthony good night.

As we drove home, Linda looked out the window and cried. She knew Anthony had to be at the hospital, that this was what was best for him. But that didn't make it easier for her to leave him behind.

CHAPTER 10

Anthony Comes Home

DECEMBER 12, 1998

It was Saturday, late afternoon. Linda had gone to the hospital while I had stayed home with Alex. Later that day I left to pick up a friend at the airport. I had worked closely with Chris Carlson a few years ago while we were both with the Cincinnati office of Provident Life and Accident, an insurance carrier. Our offices had been located in Mount Adams and we had become friends, linked by our common business goals and our routine of running mornings through the streets of Mount Adams and Eden Park. At the end of our five-mile route, we would catch our breath, and over Gatorade or a milkshake, we would sit, talking about our dreams and future plans.

When the Carlsons had lived in Cincinnati, Linda had become close friends with Chris's wife, Barb. Both our families had kids under the age of five, and Barb and Linda would get together at least once a week to hang out while the kids played. Being somewhat curtailed by our kids' young ages, the four of us regularly spent weekend evenings, birthdays and holidays together, at one home or the other, barbecuing and visiting.

Chris moved his family to Seattle, where he had lived formerly, when Provident Life and Accident closed the Cincinnati office. We had stayed in touch, remaining good friends over the five years since he had left. Chris was on a business trip, and had made arrangements to lay over in Cincinnati.

Chris's flight arrived a little after four o'clock. I met him as he came up the escalator from the gates. We exited the terminal and headed to the hospital. While we drove, Chris asked how things were going and I told him, in detail, what to expect when he saw Anthony. He knew Anthony well from the time our families had spent together and I wanted him to be prepared when he saw him.

We arrived at the hospital shortly before five. The door to Anthony's room was closed so Chris stayed outside while I went in to see what was going on. Linda was changing Anthony as I came into the room and she turned to me and said, "I can't stand this any longer. I'm tired of feeling like I'm never home. I'm sick of the hospital. I'm sick of leaving Anthony behind every day. I worry that he wakes up in this place, wondering where he is, where we are, if we love him anymore. I am on the phone at three a.m. every night, asking the nurses how he is, if he is asleep or awake. I just can't do this anymore. I want to take him home, now. Tonight."

I looked at her tortured face. Were we ready to take Anthony and all his needs on? I wondered briefly. But I was sick of the hospital too. I wanted our family together again. This was a big step, but we would figure it out somehow.

"Will they discharge him tonight?" Then I remembered. "Chris is waiting outside to say hello."

I was sure that Linda was preoccupied with her desire to take Anthony home and would rather not be visiting at that

moment, but she also knew that Chris had made special arrangements to come to town. Most people were more comfortable staying away. This scene of a perfectly normal child, now deformed and drooling, was ghastly and particularly painful to those who knew him well. It was certainly more than most wanted to see. The fact that Chris had made arrangements to visit during this trying time was touching.

She took a deep breath. "Okay."

As Chris entered, his eyes took in the bed where Anthony lay. Linda knew Chris well enough to know that he would demonstrate little emotion. An intensely private person, he preferred to maintain his distance in most relationships. He hugged Linda briefly, unable to speak. She knew that he would deal with this sad scene later, when he was alone and away from us, when his reaction wouldn't add further angst to our current state of mind.

"I want to take Anthony home tonight. It's not like the hospital is doing anything we can't do at home with the nurses and therapists that the agency will send."

It was Chris' nature to be supportive, to help people achieve their goals. He had the ability to instill confidence in those around him and he had been a good manager for this reason. "What can I do to help?" he asked.

Since Thanksgiving, we had brought Anthony home to visit a couple times. We had even kept him overnight once, so we had a medical bed delivered and installed in our family room. The social worker at the hospital had put Linda in touch with a home care agency, telling her that Children's wouldn't discharge Anthony until Medicaid and nursing support were in place. The owners of the agency had been out to assess Anthony's case and to visit with Linda. They had given her their

office and home phone numbers so that she could reach them day or night.

When Linda called their home that evening, she was told that the agency wouldn't be able to get a nurse out until Monday morning, but by this time, Linda and I were on a mission to get Anthony out of the hospital. We had made up our minds that we were taking our son home. The three of us packed clothes, gifts and cards, splints and therapy implements, medical supplies, formula and prescriptions. The doctor wrote the discharge orders that detailed his care. The nurse ordered an IV pole and feeding pump to be delivered to our home. She reviewed Anthony's medications and nutrition schedule with Linda while Chris and I loaded the car.

Before we could leave, Anthony had to be seen by the doctor on call. Mary McMahon was the most empathetic of the doctors on the floor, and we had seen her many times over the past six weeks. Calm, nurturing and unhurried, we came to prefer Dr. Mary's ability to listen and respond to us without the patronizing attitude that is sometimes present in pediatricians, who are sure they know more about your children than you do.

Dr. Mary knocked on the open door and greeted us with a smile. "So, I hear you want to take Anthony home. It is unusual for a patient like Anthony to leave so abruptly. Usually we prepare for a week to discharge a patient. However, most of that time is spent training parents on the child's care, and Linda has been involved in Anthony's care from day one, so I will make an exception in this case. We will finish up the discharge papers after I perform the final assessment and you will be on your way." She opened each of his eyelids and shone a penlight at his pupils, looking for them to dilate. She then moved it back and forth, looking for evidence that his eyes were tracking. She

checked each of his reflexes by tapping his elbows and knees gently with a rubber hammer. She listened, through the stethoscope, to his lungs and bowel sounds.

Dr. Mary asked him to touch his nose, patiently giving him time to process and respond to the request. He touched his nose. Again she asked him to touch his nose. Again he touched his nose. Again she asked. Again he touched his nose.

Linda looked at me. "Did you see that? He touched his nose!" she exclaimed. This was the first time he had been able to comply with this request, one that we had heard every day and every time a doctor had made her rounds for the past six weeks. "He did it again!" Boy, were we elated. This was real progress! He must be coming out of his coma! Surely he would be speaking and sitting up shortly.

Dr Mary explained that Anthony was "perseverating," which she described as a part of the brain's recovery process, whereby the patient gets stuck doing or saying the same thing repeatedly. But her explanation didn't douse our excitement. It was the first time he had done anything intentional in over three months.

Our discussion with Dr. McMahon lasted twenty minutes or so, and during that time Anthony continued to touch his nose. Not just a couple of times, but consistently throughout the twenty-minute conversation. Dr Mary may have thought Anthony was perseverating, but I knew him, and I knew exactly what he was doing. I had seen it before.

During the last couple of years, Anthony had played first base for our team, the Black Sox. He had quick hands and was great at anticipating where the ball would go, usually putting himself in position in the nick of time. Rarely did a ball get by him.

However, one Saturday morning at Grooms Field, when he

took his position at first base, the lead-off batter hit a line drive between Anthony and the second baseman. I'd seen Anthony make this play hundreds of times in practice and in games. But he didn't this time.

After the game I asked him. "What happened in that first play? He replied, "I just missed the ball, Dad." "Well, you can't afford to miss the ball as the starting first baseman. We'll work on it tomorrow," I promised.

In the days following the game I must have hit a hundred balls to him. He made every play, and every time he scowled at me as if to say, 'you won't find a better first baseman.' He was proving to me that he had earned this position and he could do this job.

I was sure Anthony knew what was going on. It was clear to me that he could hear us and knew he was going home. By touching his nose repeatedly, he was telling us, in the only way he was able, that he had earned the right to go home. He would do whatever it took to achieve that goal.

"Let's finish up so we can get you out of here," Dr. Mary said. To Anthony she said, "We'll miss you. But we'll see you in a couple of weeks when you're back for a checkup." He touched his nose once again, as if to say goodbye.

Somehow it all came together that night. Linda, Chris and I brought Anthony home. The feeding pump and I.V. pole were delivered. We transferred him into his medical bed and settled his things around him in the family room.

As we looked at him lying there, in his favorite spot in the family room, it was obvious that he was content. He was more peaceful that night than he had been in months. He knew he was finally home.

CHAPTER 11

The Namesake

AUGUST 4, 1986

You'd think that when your wife tells you she's going to have a baby, it wouldn't come as a surprise. After all, you've been watching her stomach grow until it looks like it will pop, accompanying her to Lamaze classes, painting walls and buying baby furniture. But maybe births, like deaths, are alike in that they always come as a surprise. Are you ever really ready for either?

About 6 a.m. Monday morning, August 4, I'm lying in bed thinking through the day ahead when Linda returns from the bathroom. As she stands next to the bed looking down at me she says eagerly, "I just heard something pop. I think we might have a baby today." "Really?" I ask. She says, "Well, we're still two weeks from the official due date so it could be a false alarm. I guess we'll find out soon enough."

She is excited, not nervous. I figure she'll let me know when and if I need to move quickly. In the meantime, I'm thinking about who I might need to call and appointments I might have to cancel as I get dressed. I am making coffee in our small kitchen when she comes in holding the phone to her ear. She is talking to the doctor's

office. When she gets off, she tells me that the doctor suggests that she be at the hospital around 8 a.m.

We knew from birthing classes that first babies usually have longer labors than those that follow, and the doctor reminded Linda that she should be active to help things move along more efficiently, so she checks to make sure she has everything she needs to take to the hospital. We clean and straighten our two bedroom condo before we leave. We stay busy making sure everything is ready and I wonder if this is the last time it will be just the two of us.

She also calls Malcolm, her boss, to let him know that she is going into labor and she will call him tomorrow. Linda started and runs the commercial division for a retail fitness chain called Busybody and has built up a large and loyal clientele in clubs and hotels. She is considered an expert in the world of Texas fitness, having been a competitive bodybuilder and a former owner of two "muscle head" gyms.

We originally met at the initial groundbreaking ceremony and kickoff for Turtle Creek, a premier facility located in Dallas, when I had come in from Kansas City to represent Nautilus Equipment. She was at the event, representing Busybody and seemed to know everybody there. We continued to run into each other at club openings and promotions, after I moved to town when I took over the Regional Sales Manager position in the Dallas office. What originally started as a business relationship, quickly turned personal when I realized she had everything I had ever looked for in a woman—she was bright, good looking and athletic. We shared common interests and goals. We fit together like the pieces of a puzzle. Well, it actually took me a couple of months to help her see the puzzle, but once I convinced her, she was in.

Malcolm Mentor is the owner of Busybody, a chain of fitness stores and depends upon Linda for all commercial fitness

transactions. They had decided that she would work from home within a couple of days after the baby is born. We now have a small office set up in our family room alongside the infant swing and the playpen. Linda expects to be back at work shortly after she gets home.

We are only five minutes from St. Paul Medical Center so we aren't worried about getting there in time. Shortly before eight o'clock, I load her and her overnight bag into my Camaro and drive the few miles that separate us from the hospital. We hold hands and talk as we drive, wondering if the baby will be a boy or a girl. Linda is still feeling fine, the contractions are still minor, and so I drop her off at the front door under the canopy so she can check in while I park the car. Shortly after I get to the receiving area we follow the nurse to the labor and delivery area, me pushing the wheelchair that hospital personnel insist Linda sit in.

A nurse sets us up in a sterile looking room, outfitted with a single size medical bed, an armchair and a TV, along with the usual sink and cabinet. She leaves after taking Linda's vital signs and noting the time between contractions, advising us that it will be a while and to push the call button if we need anything before she comes back to check on the progress. It is still early, maybe nine thirty or ten in the morning. We talk, laugh and take pictures to commemorate this big event.

Good thing we did because by about 4 p.m., Linda isn't up for the camera anymore. She is in heavy labor and has been for an hour. She has had an epidural, a shot into the back, that is supposed to numb the lower body, but because the baby's heart rate is irregular they have her lay on her left side. As a result, only half of the pain is dulled. The other half is without any painkiller at all.

From the start, Linda made it clear to the doctors that she has no intention of delivering this baby naturally, and in fact, only half jokingly, asked if they could knock her out completely. In birthing

class we would hear "natural is better for the baby," meaning whatever drug is given to the mother is passed on to the child, but Linda's take is that this event isn't easy on "junior" either. In her mind, modern medicine provides a definite benefit for both parties and is therefore all the more justified. From my perspective, whatever she wants is fine. I might joke about "wishing I could have the babies," but it is truly a joke. I can't imagine what this feels like and am glad I will never have to know.

The baby's irregular heartbeat causes some concern for the doctor and she orders a monitor be applied that will allow her to observe the pattern on a digital screen. The nurses repeatedly reposition Linda hoping they can get the baby's heart rate to stabilize. They finally have her lay on her right side and this seems to have some positive effect. But between the pain of the contractions and the stress of the fetus' unstable heart rate, Linda has dark circles around her eyes and looks a shade of grey. She is getting tired.

At about eight o'clock, twelve hours after we've checked into the hospital, the nurses help Linda transfer from the bed to a gurney and we head to the delivery room. She is exhausted from the last several hours of hard contractions, but she has been a champ, never once calling me names or cursing me, which they warn you women usually do when they are experiencing hard labor. But I am ready to get this over. Observing her in this pain is wearing on me, too. I'm relieved when they tell her to push one last time and I see and then hear the baby cry. I can see the light at the end of the tunnel. It is finally over and everything will be alright.

A rush of sheer exhilaration overwhelms me as the doctor announces, "It's a boy."

In the moment when they hand me my newborn child and I look down at his little red face, all I can do is cry. I have a son. I have a SON. I HAVE A SON.

CHAPTER 12

On the Road Again

It was 5:30 a.m. the first Monday morning after Anthony had come home from the hospital.

I had to leave to work with USI in Manchester, New Hampshire and was distractedly packing my suitcase, guiltily looking forward to getting away from this nightmare that had become my life, but paradoxically reluctant to leave.

As I finished packing, I caught sight of a photo of Anthony and me that was taken outside of the old Cincinnati Red's stadium before opening game in 1996. I was taken back to that date of April 1, 1996 remembering that John McSherry, a 25-year veteran umpire for Major League Baseball had collapsed on home plate just after yelling, "Play ball!"

Looking at this photo, I remembered how I lost Anthony that day. We had been standing, waiting for an update on the status of McSherry and the game when Anthony said he needed to go to the men's room. We were in the "nosebleed" section over right field. I pointed him in the direction of the lavatory and away he went. Shortly after he left, it was announced that

McSherry had died and the game was cancelled. Fans immediately began rushing out of the stadium, swarming the rows and aisles. I knew that nine-year-old Anthony would be trying to find me and would be panicked at the mayhem, so I headed up the stairs, head swiveling, eyes peeled looking for him. I nearly missed him, lost in the sea of red shirts and noise. I grabbed him and could see the relief in his eyes.

Not in a million years would I have guessed that I really would lose him. I was jolted, once again, by an overwhelming sense of loss. I missed him so much, missed our time together and missed what he had been growing into, that I physically ached.

I thought of the countless times I had scolded him about leaving his shoes and socks lying around, always trying to teach him neatness and order. I wondered if I would ever again have the opportunity to find these items strewn on the family room floor. If I did, would I still find this sloppy habit annoying? Ruefully, I recognized that I probably would, knowing that I believe in discipline. I believe that order is a requisite for success, and I perceive even my own sloppiness as a sign of weakness. But I also knew that I would give so much, anything I owned, for this childish habit, that I resolved to give him a pass now and then, should he recover enough to be able to take off his own shoes and leave them lying around.

As I came down the stairs with my suitcase, I looked over the banister into the family room. Anthony lay in his medical bed, still and quiet, the only noise the hum of the Kangaroo pump that fed formula directly into his stomach via a port that a gastroenterologist had placed there a couple of weeks before we left the hospital. Each time the pump cycled, it made a hushed whirring noise that changed in pitch, while it metered

the thick, opaque formula, forcing it through the tube that snaked down from a bag that hung from a hook and into Anthony's stomach.

The December morning was dark and cold. I set my suitcase down and made my way to the side of the bed. I had learned on September 8 that I would never again know, with absolute certainty, that I might see the people I loved. I recognized in that bleak moment, deep in my gut, that I might never again see my boy as he had been, that he had disappeared on the playground that Tuesday afternoon and had taken a piece of my soul with him when he left. In the throes of this heartbreaking realization, I grasped the rail to keep myself from dissolving onto the floor in a sea of despair. I resolved to always kiss my loved ones goodbye, when I left to go out of town, even if I had to waken them to do so.

I lifted Anthony's right hand and bent to kiss his palm, something I had done since he was a toddler, a ritual that had delighted him because he knew he could hold Daddy's affection in his hand, could keep this token of love safe within his palm. In his childish mind, he could open his fingers, take it out, and feel safe and warm and loved. Linda once told me that Anthony would "place" these kisses on the wall above his pillow, saving them for the next morning when he awoke.

This time, he was in a different place, a place I didn't know. I could only hope, as I kissed his palm and told him, "I love you," that this old ritual would stir memories or at least a familiar feeling in him. I hoped it would remind him that I loved him and that I would be here when he got back from the world he was currently visiting, the isolated world one inhabits in a coma.

I looked at Anthony's face and prayed, as I had done each

time I left the hospital, that by the time I returned, he would be magically restored to his former self, that twelve-year-old, storytelling, shoes-in-the-family-room, sweaty and exasperating and wonderful kid that he had been before September 8. Hoping that he would turn that corner and be back to play NFL video football with me when I returned from New England.

I had to leave, had to get to the airport, but instead I turned around, climbed the stairs and entered Alex's bedroom. She was sound asleep on her back, knees bent, her dark hair in a mess around her face and pillow. The last three months had taken a toll on her and this showed in the current disarray of her room; her clothes, toys, "dress up" costumes and books strewn about the floor.

Her brother, her only sibling living in our home, had disappeared. Her parents were either absent or preoccupied with Anthony, nursing or medical issues. She was on her own, left to figure out what to wear to school and when to put herself to bed most evenings. I wondered how deeply this drastic change in her life had affected her. I knew that she was not getting the attention she needed, but I also knew it wouldn't, couldn't change anytime soon.

Still upset as I thought about Anthony, my eyes welled up at the sight of my seven-year-old daughter, imagining the confusion, the sadness she felt. Linda mentioned that Mrs. Landis, Blue Ash Elementary's school counselor, had scheduled twice weekly meetings with Alex, recognizing that she needed attention just to maintain a semblance of emotional balance in this tragic and precarious situation. I hoped these meetings helped Alex to feel less alone.

I bent to kiss her forehead, whispering, "I love you. I'll see you in a couple days."

She moaned and rolled over in response. I'm not sure she knew I was leaving.

At the bottom of the stairs, I picked up my suitcase and headed to the kitchen where Linda sat with her planner and the nursing schedule, a cup of coffee in front of her.

We each acknowledged the other, both of us lost in a turbulent ocean of personal misery, overwhelmed by our newly acquired responsibility and worry. We were happy to have Anthony home from the hospital, but we were now primary caregivers for him. His well-being was in our hands and neither of us were confident that we knew how to care for a chronically ill child.

I paused for a second to look at her. I bent and kissed her on the cheek, perfunctorily told her that I loved her and would call her later that evening when I got to the hotel. She looked at me and, in her face, I saw that this act of my leaving was taking a tremendous toll on her. For a brief moment, I thought she would say something, but instead, she dropped her eyes and waved her hand, dismissing me. She mumbled, "I love you, too." She retreated behind the invisible wall that separated us and returned her attention to more immediate needs, numb at being left alone to deal with a life that was now shaped by Anthony's condition and a newfound fear of the unknown. What would today, tomorrow, next month and next year bring? We had no idea.

I opened the trunk of my car, put my suitcase and computer case inside, closed the trunk, and got behind the steering wheel. I stared into the kitchen through the illuminated window and whispered, "I love you."

"Focus," I told myself, as I backed out of the driveway. "Focus."

I dried the tears with the back of my hand, as I drove to the airport.

• • •

As the plane flew north, I reviewed the schedule I had arranged for this visit. Typically, our clients received a variety of services that followed a regular format once I had evaluated for the "disconnects" that usually exist between the executive team and the sales force. Each month when I visited, I delivered a group session centered on a specific topic and met with executive level and management. I also held one-on-ones, which were fifteen-minute development and accountability meetings with select salespeople.

My first meeting of the day would be a one-on-one meeting with Nate, a brokerage sales rep. I knew that Nate would expect me to empathize with his failing status relative to his goals. He would want me to plead his case to Tim, the president and sales manager. I had bad news for him. That wasn't going to happen.

I realized that one of the by-products of Anthony's heart attack was that I was less patient. Given everything I had to deal with in my attempts to juggle family, the business and my own emotional turmoil, I didn't have time to make excuses, nor was I tolerant of those who didn't want to "Just do it," to quote the Nike ad. I found myself thinking and saying, "If you don't want to get it, get out!" Intellectually, I recognized that this wasn't the best way to approach people who needed training and coaching. As an education major in college, I learned that people evolve in their learning and that there is a fine line between pushing and pulling them in a direction. But right then, I was

in the push mode and I was ready to push those who weren't willing to do the job right out the door.

I landed at the Manchester airport and was looking forward to seeing Tim, the CEO of the New England operation. As I made my way through security, Tim was waiting. When I reached him, he hugged me and started asking questions. "How is Anthony?" "How are you dealing with this?" I knew that I would get to his office and I would be asked these questions from every one of his eighteen salespeople and eighteen times I would have to recount Anthony's tragic story detail by painful detail. As I played this out in my mind, I began to feel the tension build. Every time I went through this scenario, I relived the entire event and felt the pain all over again. This day I would get to experience the heartache eighteen times.

As we drove to the corporate offices, we talked about how Linda and I were coping. I imagined he wondered how my travelling was affecting the situation at home and whether or not I would be able to continue to train clients out of town. We finally made the transition to his business, specifically what we needed to accomplish in this visit and the agenda for that day. I would conduct fifteen-minute sessions with four of the producers. At ten a.m. we would begin our group session, which would finish at five p.m. Tim and I would debrief over dinner. The next day I would meet individually with some of the other salespeople. Afterward, Tim would drive me to the airport where we would have our customary bowl of New England clam chowder and by noon I would be on my way home.

My one-on-one meetings with the four producers went as expected. Nate was not selling enough to justify his contract for too much longer. I worked with him, identifying his personal

goals, trying to get him to commit, hoping to motivate him. Sandy was doing well, but couldn't seem to grow her business. I advised her to let the agency handle her smaller accounts so that she could free up time to sell. Mickey had gotten comfortable with his income and lifestyle and I challenged him to set a new goal of qualifying for Pinnacle Club, an award trip that would acknowledge him as one of the best producers in the country. Dick had an issue with a specific client. We role-played the best way to handle it.

I had a break in the action prior to our group session. I immediately thought of home. For two hours I had pushed what had happened out of my mind, focusing on helping other people find answers to their problems. But the moment my mind was free it returned to Anthony, and I was once again consumed by my own personal, ever-present cloud of helplessness and misery.

Nothing in my bag of tricks could help my son who lay at home in a coma.

• • •

The group training session focused on goal setting and the necessity of desire and commitment.

I had always been a driven personality and, for as long as I can remember, I've had clearly defined goals and a singular focus on accomplishing them. I remember when I was nine; I decided to play football. As I ran off the field that first day, my dad asked me how I liked it. I told him that I loved it and that I would go to college and play someday.

We both knew I would have to do this on my own. As a foreman for a blueberry farm, my dad couldn't afford to pay for

college. He told me that if I really wanted to play I would have to be in great shape. "Take off your shoulder pads and run another two miles." For the next eight years I played Pop-Warner football and then went on to become a more than average center for the Hammonton High School football team. My hard work paid off as I entered college at the University of Connecticut on a full football scholarship.

Goals like this are what drive us. The goals we set in our hearts, the goals that we identify as non-negotiable, and the goals that we must accomplish come hell or high water. These are the goals that keep us alive.

As I thought about Anthony and our initial goals of getting him to his first junior high dance while he lay in bed in a coma, I knew that they were born of ignorance. I had no idea that his brain injury was so devastating that the first session with his speech therapist would involve her touching his lips with an ice cube, hoping to get him to use his tongue to locate the stimulus. I thought he would be sitting up and talking and eating within a couple of days of his heart attack.

But, my football career didn't happen overnight, either. I had to learn basic skills. I had to train hard and consistently. I had to study the game intimately. I had to develop my abilities over time. I resolved to push Anthony for as long and hard as it took to make him whole again.

After the group training session, while Tim finished in his office, I called home to see how things had gone my first day out of town since September 8. Grandma answered the phone and told me that an ambulance had taken Anthony and Linda back to Children's Hospital per the new homecare nurse's orders. Apparently, Anthony was still vomiting and she was concerned that he would aspirate, causing pneumonia. She wanted the

hospital to X-ray him to check the placement of the feeding tube, thinking it may have been dislodged.

Not a good way to start off. I knew that my absence during this episode was precarious and left Linda to carry this burden alone. But I knew we didn't have any options currently. We both knew it. I had travelled a lot during the past five years because most of our clients were located out of town. I also knew Linda was quite capable of handling things alone. She always had been. She had done it for the five years while I was on the road before Anthony got sick. She had been with him throughout all of his procedures and therapies at the hospital. She had made all the arrangements to get him home. She would figure it out.

I knew I was justifying my absence to soothe my conscience. I also knew that I was relieved not to be in the midst of Anthony's latest incident. The last three months of my life had been consumed by his status, his medical tests and his all-encompassing needs. I was looking forward to having dinner and a conversation that had nothing to do with CT scans, brain injuries and therapies. I would call Linda later. In the meantime there was nothing I could do.

Tim and I headed out for dinner. We usually went to C.R. Sparks, which is located in the quaint town of Bedford, New Hampshire, just west of the USI office. We talked as Tim drove, catching up on what had happened that day, singling out the producers that needed special attention, pinpointing issues that needed to be addressed in the next training session, strategizing about which one of us would be most effective in dealing with certain situations.

It was already dark when we arrived at the restaurant. Several cars in the parking lot on this cold wintry night indicated a few hardy souls had sought happy hour in the comfort of the

warm New England interior of Sparks. As we entered, I was enveloped in the aroma of fine food and a welcoming casual ambience created by dark wood, brick and stone. From the entry, I saw several chefs in the exhibition style kitchen that lay just beyond the marble serve top.

Tim and I sat at a table covered by a checkered cloth and ordered appetizers. Over a glass of wine I asked him, "How much longer are you going to accept mediocrity from a third of your sales staff?"

It was my job to help sales organizations increase revenue. I had been gone for several months and I needed to help Tim move this organization forward or he would be unable to justify the expense of my services. The frustration I felt about Anthony and the fact that I was making up for lost time were making me even more direct than usual.

• • •

Later that evening, Linda told me that the emergency room doctor had recommended that we have Anthony's saliva glands cut so that he would no longer deal with normal oral secretions. She was appalled that they would suggest such drastic action and refused to consider this option. The good news is that the entire trip to the hospital took only three hours. Apparently, the ambulance drivers were sympathetic to Linda's situation and informed her that they weren't going to take any calls until they got her and Anthony home. So, what could have been a long and drawn out six to eight-hour event turned into a much less stressful situation. I was relieved that Linda was dealing with everything well without me.

Sitting in the hotel room, I remembered the past summer,

only six months ago, when I was coaching the Black Sox base-ball team. I told Anthony, who was up to bat, that he needed to hit a double to get Billy to home plate so we could win the game and go to the playoffs. He did it. He got the job done. He always did. I remembered his smile in the hospital, when he rec-ognized our private joke about pig's legs and flapjacks. I was positive that he was "in there" and would be okay when he came out of his coma. As the doctors advised, we simply had to work hard at keeping his physical condition from deteriorating until he woke up and began to use his arms and legs. I resolved to renew my efforts and those of the nurses and therapists when I got home.

On the return flight, I wrote my follow-up memo to Tim summarizing the training session and one-on-ones with each of the salespeople, noting that several of them needed to adjust their behaviors or get out of selling. In the process, I mentally related the teachings to my personal context of Anthony. My commitment to working him harder meant all staff must ac-cept a "no excuses" mentality. I planned out my next several therapy sessions which reflected my revitalized pledge.

CHAPTER 13

A Heartbreaking Christmas

DECEMBER 1998

Coming home from New Hampshire was difficult. For the first time in months, I had left behind the everyday reminders of my loss. While I was on the road, I would experience moments when I was flooded by an inconsolable sadness. But shortly the waters would recede and soon my mind would address more pressing issues. The situation didn't seem quite so real when I wasn't face to face with it. I found that while I was busy with clients I could temporarily forget about Anthony. I could forget about the drastic changes in my life and in my family. Being home again brought it all back.

Nothing had prepared me for this traumatic return. My brain couldn't accept Anthony's tragedy or my inability to affect his situation. While out of town I was able to build enthusiasm and plan for his therapy sessions. I could imagine Anthony responding to my coaching as he had always done. But once I was home, in the light of his reality, my plans collapsed. The thinking person that was Anthony had disappeared; his body was an empty shell, incapable of responding to any request. In the past

three months we had witnessed purposeful actions only a couple of times; once when he smiled at my pig's legs story and once during the discharge exam when he touched his nose. We hadn't seen anything since then.

But there was good news. He was finally home with us. Our family was together again. Even though our lifestyle had been drastically altered, Linda didn't have to be at Children's Hospital every day. She could take care of Anthony in the comfort of our home.

Anyone who has spent an extended period of time at a hospital knows how tiresome and disruptive this schedule is to one's life. This is particularly true when kids are involved because parents and patient are uncomfortable being separated. While the nurses at Children's did an amazing job of nurturing our family, particularly Linda and Anthony during his three-month stay, we were happy to be out of the sterile, institutional environment.

While I was away on business, the nursing agency had called to tell Linda they were sending an RN for her to interview as Anthony's primary nurse. Linda met with Gail and decided that she was perfect for the job. Experienced, energetic and resourceful, Gail cured Anthony's nausea within hours of her visit by suggesting that Linda replace his current formula with Ensure nutritional supplement which she could get at the grocery. Linda followed Gail's instructions and within twenty-four hours Anthony was noticeably better. After six weeks of vomiting, we stopped worrying about the possibility of him developing pneumonia from aspiration. Linda called the agency and asked to keep Gail long term.

Soon Anthony had a staff of nurses who knew him well, each of them trained on his medical and physical issues and

committed to his rehabilitation. Simultaneously, Linda and the agency arranged for visiting therapists to pick up where the hospital had left off. Between the homecare nurses and therapists and the personnel sent by Sycamore Schools, our house soon became a hub of activity.

Anthony's condition, however, had not improved. He still lay comatose and unresponsive. Linda and I had prayed that he would be miraculously restored, that being in a familiar setting would touch something deep inside him, that one morning, afternoon or evening he would "wake up" and ask for something to eat. But that hadn't happened. He had changed very little over the past several weeks and we felt desperate.

It had been a long time since I had last seen the unique personality of my son and, while I told myself that he would be alright, I was beginning to have moments of doubt. I had seen no sign that he was "in there" since the time he touched his nose for Dr. McMahon when she examined him before allowing us to take him home. Each day that passed meant one more day without him. Void of emotion, thought or ability, Anthony was a different person, no longer the boy I had known and loved. I had visions of him while he lie on the playground, his spirit separating from his body, looking sadly down at his own form, recognizing he would never inhabit it again and wondering what had gone so wrong. Wondering if he would ever again know the carefree life of a normal seventh grader. Wondering if he would ever again see his mom and dad.

One night Linda asked me to throw a load of laundry in the washer. As I entered the laundry room, I saw a pile of stuff, including get well cards and balloons, framed pictures, a scrapbook, posters and stuffed animals, that we had brought home from the hospital with us that Saturday night. As I sorted

through it I found a white plastic bag with a drawstring knotting the opening. I tried to untie the string but instead resorted to ripping the bag open. A strong odor of urine assailed me. What the heck was this? Surely the hospital wouldn't send us home with dirty linens.

I dumped the contents onto the floor. Anthony's high top Nike basketball shoes tumbled out. These shoes had been a source of pride to him because they were endorsed by Michael Jordan. He was sure that they added to his prowess on the court and he had spent hours on the driveway shooting hoops and pretending to be this famous and charismatic talent.

As I shook the plastic bag, the t-shirt, shorts and socks he had been wearing on September 8, fell to the floor. Picking up the t-shirt, I saw the dark splotches of his dried blood resulting from the abrasion on his face when he fell. Sadly, I noticed the familiar spot just below the left shoulder where he used his shirt as a towel to dry his sweaty upper lip. Something that drove Linda crazy, all his t-shirts had a dark smudge from this little habit that even Clorox couldn't erase. I winced when I saw the shirt, underwear and shorts, ripped from top to bottom where the EMTs had sliced them open.

These souvenirs took me back to the place and time of his accident. I was shocked, unprepared to face the reality of his horrendous experience. My mind returned to that day, that moment in his young life. Overcome by what he went through on the playground that Tuesday afternoon, I melted to the floor and cried silently amidst these soiled tokens of him. Too painful for me to relive, I prayed to God that he lost consciousness quickly so that he didn't know the agony of suffocating or the terrible electrical currents caused by the defibrillator.

Later, after I had cried out everything I had stored away for

the last several months, I threw his clothes and shoes, everything except his ruined leather belt, into the washer. Something inside me wanted to keep these precious pieces of his life.

Anthony had been through a lot in the past three months including dozens of hospital procedures, some without anesthesia. With any luck his future would be less painful than the recent past.

We decided to try Hyperbaric Oxygen Therapy. HBOT was expensive and difficult to implement, but we were committed to doing everything in our power to restore our son. I looked into home units. Pricey, at thirty thousand dollars, and dangerous because of the pressurized oxygen. We opted to take Anthony to one of two facilities located in our area. Unfortunately, University Hospital wouldn't take Anthony as a patient since HBOT was not an approved treatment for brain injury. The other hospital was Kettering and they agreed to take Anthony for treatments, but *only* after the process had been initiated by another HBOT facility. So, we arranged to take Anthony to Hyperbaric Associates in Boca Raton, Florida. Since the center was associated with Richard Neubauer, the pioneer of HBOT as treatment for brain injury, we figured the center had experience with Anthony's type of patient and would have established a protocol that might translate into improvement in his condition.

The head of the rehabilitation department at Children's Hospital would not authorize HBOT for Anthony, citing a lack of proven results with this outside-the-box treatment. She was concerned that we might jeopardize his health by taking him beyond the hospital's reach. We had to find another solution, since Hyperbaric Associates required a doctor's authorization for treatment. Dr. Franz, Anthony's neurologist, felt that HBOT

wouldn't hurt him, but didn't offer any positive feedback. Perhaps he recognized that we had set this course and nothing would dissuade us from it.

Linda appealed to Dr. Lichtenberg, Anthony's long-time pediatrician, to help. Although her manner could be gruff, Ann Lichtenberg was empathetic to our case. Once she saw Anthony at her office, she recognized that we had nothing to lose. She saw the pleading hope in Linda's eyes and decided that HBOT would not harm Anthony. She agreed to write the necessary orders. It took Linda more than a month to arrange doctor's appointments, medical tests, flights, equipment and living arrangements for the trip which would take place in January.

The holidays were a blur. My dad, who lived in up-state New York with my mom, had an aneurysm that put him in the hospital and nearly killed him. I was unable to visit because of Anthony and only heard via my brother, Michael, how he was doing. While I was concerned about Dad, I was so caught up in all the sadness and chaos in my own life that I was unable to assimilate the severity of his emergency. There was simply no room in my head for more tragedy.

My father-in-law had been on kidney dialysis for years and was getting noticeably weaker. I suspected that Anthony's disappearance exacerbated his deteriorating condition. Grandpa had been Anthony's biggest fan from the time we had moved to Cincinnati from Dallas, carrying him around the house as a baby, following him for hours as he explored their yard as a toddler, attending nearly all of his games, even when walking became difficult for him. He and Grandma had kept Anthony at least once a week for nearly ten years. The tragic disappearance of Anthony's personality left a gaping hole in their lives.

I busied myself stringing outdoor lights and putting up the

Christmas tree. This annual tradition of preparing for the holidays usually filled me with happiness, but my enthusiasm had disappeared, along with my annual helpmate, my son. I numbly went through the motions of last minute decorating trying to create some semblance of normalcy for Alex's sake.

On Christmas Eve, Linda's brothers and their families came to town just like they always did. Grandma made a traditional holiday meal of turkey, mashed potatoes, stuffing and pumpkin pie, which we all ate while sitting around our big dining room table. Linda's brothers and their wives were overwhelmed upon seeing Anthony and our conversation was less than the usual banter. But we were optimistic about HBOT and the results we had seen on the promotional video. We were certain this treatment would bring about big changes in Anthony's condition.

That night, after everyone left, Linda read "The Night Before Christmas," which Anthony had been able to recite from memory, having heard it countless times over the years. Seven-year-old Alex lay in the medical bed next to him, pulling tabs and opening the windows of the worn pop-up book, a gift that Linda had given Anthony when he was two. Alex then slept on the sofa next to her brother's bed, as she had done in years past. It was customary for the two of them to spend Christmas Eve night in this room, hoping to see Santa.

I went to bed praying for a miracle, a present that wouldn't fit in my stocking or under the Christmas tree.

CHAPTER 14

Florida and HBOT

JANUARY 3, 1999

Soon the holidays were over and Linda's brothers returned to their homes. We were caught up in arrangements for our upcoming trip to Florida. Linda shipped cartons of supplies to the condominium location and ordered a rented medical bed and a feeding pump to be delivered and set up in our unit. Alex would stay with Aunt Jeni, Grandma and Grandpa while Linda and I got Anthony to Florida. In a week, after we had started HBOT, Jeni and Alex would come down to be with Linda while I flew to Philadelphia to meet with a prospective client.

Travelling with Anthony in a comatose state was a monumental undertaking, and we were doing it without nursing assistance. Perhaps, we should have questioned whether taking him out of the care of his nurses and doctors at this time was a good idea. But, the HBOT experts were adamant that the sooner treatment was initiated, the better the chances were of optimizing Anthony's recovery. We had already lost three months while Anthony was in the hospital and another month because Hyperbaric Associates refused to take him until after

the holidays. We were now four months out from his initial brain trauma and we were losing the precious early treatment window that the HBOT experts preferred.

I cashed in frequent flyer miles for first-class tickets, knowing we'd need the more spacious seating to accommodate Anthony. Just getting him on and off an airplane was going to be a production since he couldn't walk. In fact, getting him in and out of a car went like this: I stood Anthony, who was 5'7" and 130 pounds, next to the open front passenger side door of the car and swiveled him so that his rear was lined up with the seat and slowly lowered him into the car. Meanwhile, Linda, who was in the backseat, stabilized his body, keeping it upright until he was seated. I moved his feet onto the floor of the car. Once Anthony was in the car, we shifted him back so that he was properly aligned and we could fasten his seatbelt. At this early stage, Children's had given us a special harness that, when used with a standard seat and chest belt, served to stabilize his upper body.

At the airport we transferred him from the car to one of the Delta wheelchairs so that his own wheelchair could be placed in cargo. Before boarding the plane, we settled him in a narrow aisle wheelchair, which provided extra strapping to keep him from falling over. We used the aisle wheelchair to move him from the gate to his seat inside the plane. I then moved him into the airplane seat while Linda stabilized his upper body from behind. Next we picked him up and moved him to the window seat. This optimal position allowed one of us to attend to him while the wall of the cabin supported his other side.

Linda gave Anthony Ensure Plus and his medications through the g-tube port in his stomach while in-flight. He was at risk for dehydration unless we kept him on the rigid fluid

and feeding schedule detailed in his Plan of Care. This Plan of Care, which had come home from the hospital with him, was a detailed accounting of every medicine, fluid and nutritional supplement dose and time of administration. It was vital to maintaining his physical health. We followed it closely, knowing that we were outside the comfort zone of his nursing staff and Cincinnati Children's Hospital personnel who knew him so well.

When we arrived at the West Palm Beach airport, I retrieved the rental car and the same process of moving Anthony began again. He rode in the front seat on the way to our rented condo in Delray Beach.

It was dark by the time we found the condominium complex and placed Anthony in the medical bed which sat in the family room of the unit. By this time he was thoroughly agitated and "storming" again. We knew that he was fatigued from sitting up and travelling most of the day. We gave him a sedative that had been prescribed then hooked him up to the feeding pump. Linda was worried that we had put Anthony through too much at this early stage and got up several times during the night to check on him.

The following morning we gave Anthony the bed bath usually performed by his home care nurses. We brushed his teeth with a bit of mouthwash, having learned in the hospital that the abrasives in toothpaste could leave grit behind that was destructive to the soft tissues of the mouth and throat. Since Anthony couldn't rinse or swallow, we used a swab to sponge any excess mouthwash or water left behind. After stretching his legs and arms, an important routine performed twice daily to keep his muscles from shortening and limiting his range, we dressed him in clean diapers and clothes.

We arrived mid-morning at the clinic, which was located in a beautiful, newly developed office complex in Boca Raton, for our appointment. We filled out paperwork and met with one of the clinic's physicians who briefly examined Anthony, reviewed his records and asked us many questions. He studied the PET scan (Positron Emission Tomography), that the clinic required, which produced a three dimensional image of Anthony's brain. The purpose of the test was to establish a baseline of the current state of his brain activity and the levels and location of damage.

The prior week, we had taken Anthony to University Hospital, the only local hospital in our provider network that would perform the test where a solution containing a tracing element had been injected into his bloodstream. We had waited over an hour for the tracer to reach its destination, Anthony's brain, before they had placed him inside the CT X-ray scan unit for the images. It had been another in a series of long and arduous days.

The doctor set up a schedule of two-a-day HBOT treatments, the accepted protocol for patients with brain injury. While he didn't prescribe any medications, the doctor gave us a list of supplements that we should give Anthony to enhance brain function, including CoQ10, L-carnitine, Phosphatidylserine and DHA, which contains Omega 3 fatty acids.

There were two HBOT treatment options available at the clinic. One allowed several patients to sit together inside a large chamber for the prescribed "dive" time, which helped defray the cost by spreading it amongst the group. The other was a mono-chamber, which accommodated only one patient. Since Anthony was unable to sit up, we planned to use the mono chamber at a cost of two hundred dollars per treatment. To our surprise and elation just before we left, Jeni and the family gave

Linda a check for ten thousand dollars. They had pooled their money to help us finance the trip and medical expenses. It meant so much to us. As happy as we were with their amazing gift of much needed dollars, it barely dented the mountain of expenses the insurance company refused to cover.

We were escorted to the treatment area where we met Ruiz, a doctor technician from Brazil, who explained the process. Following his directions, Linda and I transferred Anthony to the vinyl covered cot that sat on a track at the head of the chamber opening. Since only cotton clothing was recommended inside, we removed all of Anthony's clothing and covered him with a sheet provided by the clinic. Ruiz pushed the bed into the chamber, closed and locked the door and began pressuring the tank with oxygen.

Ruiz explained that he would begin the treatment regimen gradually, allowing Anthony's body time to adjust to the change in pressure inside the chamber. Over the next several days, he would increase the oxygen within the tank until he reached the prescribed optimal level. Each dive would consist of a timed descent and ascent, which would help Anthony to tolerate the pressure without the side effects that scuba divers experience with drastic atmospheric changes.

We could see Anthony through the clear Plexiglas casing of the mono-chamber and we watched his face closely to make sure he was experiencing no discomfort throughout his first dive. During conversations with Hyperbaric Associates, Linda had learned that Anthony's eardrums could explode from the pressure inside the HBOT chamber if Anthony didn't swallow periodically. Since we weren't sure he was capable of this, she had taken him to Children's Hospital and had his eardrums pierced by an ear, nose and throat specialist.

We were able to talk to him via a microphone that transmitted through speakers near his head. These speakers also piped in sound from a VCR, so a patient could hear and watch a movie on the TV screen that was positioned over the chamber. We watched him closely, looking for signs that he was responding, but saw none. However, he seemed to tolerate the treatment well. Beyond his being a bit sweaty from the warm temperature inside, we saw no negative side effects. Later that day, Anthony had his second treatment.

We had planned to take Anthony back to the condo each day to lay him down and take the pressure off his backside, change his diaper, and give him liquid supplement. But by the third day we found we didn't have time to go back to the condo between HBOT sessions scheduled at ten in the morning and two in the afternoon. Soon his treatment time, including descent and ascent, took an hour and a half. Since the condo was nearly twenty minutes from the clinic, it was twelve thirty and several transfers later before he was in his bed. After those first couple days, we hung out in the parking lot, borrowed an empty room inside the clinic or walked outside to kill time until Anthony was due for his second treatment.

While walking around the complex we found Physical Therapy Centers of America, located on the opposite side of the building. This was convenient since we had been told that patients receiving HBOT demonstrated best results if treatments were combined with therapy. We scheduled Anthony for a daily session in between dives. Louis, the center manager, was a certified Neuro-Developmental Treatment (NDT) physical therapist and taught us about the connection between the brain and the body. We learned how to stimulate certain muscle groups that would trigger a response in other muscle groups.

We learned how a gentle rocking motion would relax Anthony. We learned a new neurologically based approach to therapy for Anthony.

It may have been wishful thinking, but it was during those half-hour sessions that I was sure I saw glimpses of my former son. Anthony would try to do anything Louis asked of him, whether it was move an arm or blink his eyes. Even though he couldn't talk and couldn't focus his eyes, he was a sweaty mess from effort by the end of each session. I became convinced that somewhere inside him, unnoticeable to the outside world, Anthony was working hard to come back to us.

To keep ourselves busy and to maximize the effects of HBOT we found different diversions. Between sessions we fed him through his g-tube and changed his diapers. Knowing Anthony liked to eat, we focused on helping him use his mouth and tongue again. At the grocery, Linda found Pixie Sticks, paper straws filled with a strong fruit flavored powder. We began to put small amounts of the powder on his tongue. This would stimulate his saliva glands and he had to work his mouth and swallow to accommodate the resulting oral secretions. One day we cut his toenails while sitting in the parking lot.

Every day when we got back to the condo, we would put Anthony in bed for a rest and hook him up to the feeding pump. After a couple of hours, we would stretch his limbs and rotate his joints, loosening him up for his next workout. We would then get him out of bed and have him sit Indian style, with his legs crossed, one of us sitting behind to support his back. We also had him sit with his legs straight out in front of him. These positions helped him maintain his flexibility.

We would then stand him up, one of us supporting him on either side, so that he bore weight down through his legs and

feet. This helped to prevent his feet from becoming curled up and useless, which happens naturally to patients who are bed bound and not getting up to stand or walk. Anthony's spasticity kept his left leg locked. His right leg and both arms were retracted and so to stand him, we used the splint the hospital had cast to keep his right leg straight. He had little to no control over any part of his body and a muscle contraction was more a result of his brain injury than a proactive movement on his part. But since Anthony could bear weight while supported, we were able to transfer him using his feet as a base to pivot. We needed his lower extremities to maintain their muscle tone and functionality for this purpose. Otherwise we would have to use a Hoyer lift, a bulky contraption on wheels that is used to move patients who cannot stand, each time we wanted to transfer him.

After an hour, we would put him back in bed for the night. He wasn't accustomed to being up the six-plus hours his HBOT and therapy schedule required, since at the hospital and at home, he rested between hour-long therapy sessions. This new regimen was taxing for him. He also needed hydration and nutrition, which required that he be on the feeding pump for at least twelve hours a day.

One day, upon returning to the condo complex after a day of HBOT and physical therapy, we found the elevator wasn't working and would be out of commission for at least twenty-four hours. Since our unit was on the third floor, Linda and I would have to carry Anthony up the stairs. I was furious. I had recently become aware of how much of the world was not handicap accessible and we seemed to encounter this nearly every time we left home.

I remember standing at the bottom of the stairwell,

thinking about our challenges. As if we didn't have enough already. We were tired. We were irritable. We were sad. None of this was easy or pleasant. Each and every action we took was a reminder of why we were here—Anthony's tragic condition. We had become robots just going through the motions. Neither of us had time or energy to expend beyond attending Anthony's immediate needs. We had both receded into our own private space and held ourselves in check at all times. Conversation allowed for connection, which led to vulnerability. And both of us already felt too raw and emotionally exposed. We had sealed ourselves off from the other. Wrapped in this impervious armor, we were each able to function.

Finally, we decided to carry him up the stairs. From behind I wrapped my arms under his armpits and around his chest, like they had taught me at the hospital. Linda took his legs and I backed up the stairs. At each landing, we stopped for a moment to catch our breath. I jokingly informed Anthony he needed to go on a diet. Linda chuckled ruefully when I told God aloud "If Anthony is going to walk again, this would be a good time for him to start." There was no answer so onward we trudged step after step. We got him into bed and then I went and brought up his wheelchair. The good news is that the elevator was working by the next morning.

On Saturday, January 9, I picked Jeni and Alex up at the West Palm Beach airport after dropping Linda and Anthony off for HBOT. It was Saturday and Anthony would receive one treatment. His only day off was Sunday and we let him rest, getting him up for his two-a-day improvised therapy sessions. That evening the five of us headed to a cafe, with outdoor seating, just down the street.

Unaccustomed to seeing someone in a coma, people stared

at Anthony, or they would look at him and quickly look away. I'm sure they wondered what was wrong. He drooled and his head lay to one side, nearly on his chest. There was no life in his eyes. But we wanted him to be with us. We didn't want to leave him behind just because he didn't look like the rest of us. We were adamant that we would make his life as normal as possible in the hopes that he would feel like he did prior to his cardiac arrest and then come back to this world. So we included him in everything we possibly could.

We had talked to Anthony nonstop in the hospital, telling him about different events, or showing him photos from his past. We talked to him as though he understood, asked him questions, did our best to treat him as if he weren't in a coma. We included him in conversations and pointed to things that might be of interest.

But it wasn't easy, seeing people stare at my son, formerly a typical twelve-year-old who had been an athlete and a favorite with the girls at school. It took me some time to get accustomed to being in public with Anthony. I resented that Anthony was a spectacle even while I understood people meant him no harm. I wondered if a t-shirt sporting "Brain injury due to lack of oxygen during cardiac arrest" would be legible and might alleviate some of the unwanted attention by explanation.

Jeni drove me to the airport early Monday morning. I was meeting with Doug Kreitzberg, the CEO for USI's Philadelphia offices and a prospect for our training services. I had to qualify and close this deal. It meant about fifty thousand dollars in revenue to us and I was feeling financial pressure. We needed the business. Anthony's medical bills were over two hundred and fifty thousand dollars and the health insurance company was still refusing to pay. In addition, we had new expenses for

supplies including Anthony's diapers, bed pads, gloves and formula that were adding to our stress.

I prepped for the interview while on the plane, identifying my critical questions, what Doug's responses might be and how I would handle any curve balls that could get thrown my way. My meeting with Doug was successful. We had had prior conversations and he was already familiar with my process and the program. He committed to evaluating and training his sales team. I flew back to Florida to finish HBOT and take the family home.

We searched for signs that Anthony was benefitting from treatment. He remained unreachable, unresponsive. Ruiz said he never saw this; that patients always demonstrated some positive changes within the first twenty treatments. All our efforts seemed useless, but we would go home and continue treatment at Kettering Hospital in the hopes that another twenty treatments would improve his condition.

On Sunday, January 17, while we were in the West Palm Beach airport waiting for our flight, a woman approached to tell us what a good looking boy Anthony was. I looked at him. She was right. He had always been a handsome kid, blond haired with hazel eyes. He looked like my brother, Ray, and sister, Tresa. Even in a coma, he was handsome.

We flew home and settled Anthony into his bed in the family room. Grandma and Grandpa were already there with dinner. They had missed us and were hoping to see major changes in Anthony's condition. Like us, they had prayed for a miracle. Like us, they were sorely disappointed. Like us, they didn't show it. Like us, they didn't want to add to the consuming sadness we all felt.

The next day, January 18, was Linda's birthday. In her

family, birthdays were celebrated on the Sunday closest to the actual day. Sunday dinner was a weekly event and all family members in town attended. A custom I enjoyed, the normalcy helped us cope during tough times.

We sang "Happy Birthday" to Linda, ate cake and fed Anthony a little mint chocolate chip ice cream, his favorite. Her birthday was really the next day, but I had to leave for New York City early in the morning to work with a client.

It wasn't a happy day, but we had made the trip to Florida and back without harming Anthony. And although he hadn't shown any significant signs of improvement, we had learned a lot in stepping outside our comfort zone of homecare nursing. We had proven to ourselves that we could handle Anthony and all his needs for a short time.

CHAPTER 15

Linda's Not-So-Happy Birthday

JANUARY 18, 1999

The alarm sounded at five o'clock, waking me from a restless sleep. As I rolled over to turn it off, I realized we had made it through another night with Anthony at home. It had been a little over a month since he had been discharged from the hospital and life had changed drastically once again. Nearly every detail of our existence had been affected. We were 24/7 with Anthony, always on duty. The bills from Anthony's months of medical care kept accumulating. The mounting pressure caused Linda and me to be edgy. I shook my head as I remembered how easy our lives were just six months ago when everyone was healthy. I looked back, thinking how happy we had been and how much I had taken for granted. You never know what you are missing until it is gone. I took a deep breath, sat up and put my feet on the floor.

No time to think about that now. I had a plane to catch. I showered, shaved and drank a cup of coffee. I gave Linda a kiss and quietly let myself out of the bedroom, hoping that she would sleep a little longer. The cheerless, stress filled days of coping with Anthony's absence and the longing to see him again

had stolen her sleep. She had spent many nights awake, watching over him, wondering if we would be able to afford to take care of him. She worried about all of it.

We had celebrated Linda's forty-third birthday the night before because I would be in New York City for three days. Dave Eslick, second in command at USI, had recommended that all current offices hire me to jump-start their newly acquired sales teams, and within a year I had begun working at locations in New Hampshire, Philadelphia, Cincinnati and New York.

I let myself into Alex's bedroom and kissed her goodbye. I stopped briefly to say goodbye to Anthony, who was in a trance. I looked into his empty eyes and rubbed his head. I didn't tell him that I was still in shock over what had happened to him. I didn't want him to know that I wasn't sure how things would turn out. I was certain he would have been disappointed to hear that Dad didn't know how to fix this situation.

Instead, I said the same thing I always did when I left: "I have to leave town for a few days. You're the man of the house until I get back. You take care of Mom and Alex while I'm gone, okay?" I leaned down and kissed him on the palm of his hand, lingered a moment longer hoping for a response, any kind of response. When none came, I turned and headed to the garage.

After an uneventful flight I checked into my room at the Doral Park Avenue Hotel. Suddenly I remembered that today was actually Linda's birthday. I called her, knowing that by this time she would have been up for several hours.

"Happy Birthday. I didn't want to wake you up to tell you earlier. I figured I'd call after I got here," I said.

She was quiet for a second. "It's not so happy. Dad died just after midnight."

I felt like someone had punched me in the stomach. "Oh God." Linda and her dad were really close. "What happened?"

"Jeni came over this morning to tell me. After Mom and Dad got home last night he had trouble breathing. Mom called the ambulance and they took him to Bethesda North. He must have lost consciousness because she never saw him alive again. His heart gave out while they were working on him."

"I'm so sorry. I'll cancel my session. I'll get a flight back today," I promised.

"Tony, the funeral won't be for a couple days and there isn't anything you can do here. You've already missed a lot of training in New York because of Anthony. You should stay there. We can't afford to lose that account. Don't worry about me. I'm okay," she said. She amazed me with her strength, as she had nearly every day for the last four months.

She convinced me to stay. I knew Jim Butler, the CEO, would understand if I cancelled, but I felt like I had been absent for too long already. I was trying to catch up on material that should have been delivered a couple months ago. The salespeople needed the techniques in the field. It would make a difference in their results. I knew also that my presence held people accountable. Even in this early stage, I would make a difference in the organization's performance, but I had to be there in person to adequately affect each individual's behavior.

When I got to the offices, Jim welcomed me and asked how Anthony was doing. Jim Butler is a true family man and devout Catholic. He and his wife have three girls and a boy. He had met Linda at a couple USI events and when I told him about her dad dying last night, he insisted that I leave immediately. After much back and forth I convinced him that there was nothing I could do at home right now; that Linda

had encouraged me to stay. We agreed we would get through today and I would catch a flight home that night. The half-day originally scheduled for the following day would take place next month.

That evening as I waited for the plane to take off, I thought about my thirteen-year relationship with Bob, Linda's dad. While he had never been an affectionate person, he had welcomed me into the family, making me feel a part of his world. He was reserved and like most Cincinnatians of German heritage, he worked hard. He provided very well for his family, putting Linda and her three siblings through college and investing for his retirement. He made sure Linda's mom, Pat, and the kids had everything they needed.

Bob was a private person. Not one to show his emotions, he was enamored with Anthony, who was nine months old when we moved from Dallas to Cincinnati. He positively glowed when they were together and it was almost as if they had a language that only the two of them understood. Breakfast on barstools at Frisch's countertop had recently become a regular event on the Saturday mornings that Anthony didn't have a game, and Bob had started taking Anthony fishing in the pay pond up the street from his and Grandma's condo. He loved to see Anthony's excitement at reeling in a catch. Actually, he loved to see Anthony do anything.

Anthony's heart attack and brain injury had devastated everyone. But I felt, when Bob realized at Linda's birthday party that the boy he knew and loved hadn't returned from Florida, he had lost his will to live. I was certain that the overwhelming grief of losing Anthony had killed him. Bob had died of a broken heart when this light of his life had disappeared.

I looked back and realized that each step we had taken; all

the efforts we had expended on Anthony's behalf had made no difference in his condition. At first, I thought he would be okay when he "woke up" from his coma because that's what I knew from movies. Then, when his heart was ablated, I thought he would be "fixed." Next, I was convinced he would turn the corner when he got into the rehab unit, and when that didn't do anything, I was sure HBOT would restore him. Nothing had worked to bring him back. It was as though someone had erased his brain. He was gone.

I got home late, to find Linda in the kitchen going through the mail. She was numb. Numb, from missing her son and now, from losing her dad. She had worked tirelessly at finding a cure for Anthony's condition. She had kept our family together, had kept us looking toward the future. Somehow she had managed to be strong through it all. I wondered if this would unravel her amazing fortitude.

She put her arms around me and laid her head on my chest. As I hugged her, I cried, knowing how much her dad's death added to her misery, knowing I was powerless to do anything to help. Bob had been on kidney dialysis for years and it had been hard on him, sapping his energy, his appetite and his vitality.

But on the days he hadn't been in dialysis, he and Linda spent hours together. Bob had owned a small vending business that supplemented his retirement income and together he and Linda serviced the machines. In the summer months, they often took Anthony and Alex to Sharon Woods to play in the water park, or to the zoo, or Sawyer Point down by the Ohio River. For the last year or so, he had been helping us at the office, working on our marketing plan and duplicating the audio materials that our clients received.

Bob had been ill for so long that we had become accustomed to his occasionally weakened state. He had recovered from various physical setbacks and Linda loved to tell about her dad walking into the dining room to surprise her, several months after the doctors told him he would never walk again. Bob didn't complain. He was a positive person and, if he wasn't feeling well, he didn't let on. He didn't want to cast a pall on our time together as a family. His death caught us by surprise, despite his health problems.

"I'm so sorry about your dad. I wish there was something I could do," I whispered into her hair.

Linda was quiet for a long time, and then she said, "He figured he couldn't do anything here to help so he went to the top. He's in heaven begging God to send Anthony home to us."

The next day, while sitting in the kitchen after school, we told both kids about Grandpa. Alex was young. At seven years old, it was her first experience with death and she didn't totally understand. She was sad, but soon moved on to other things, asking if she could go and play with Natalie next door.

Anthony was sitting in his wheelchair, seemingly unaffected by the discussion. After Alex left, Linda got up close to his ear and said softly, "Anthony, Grandpa died yesterday. You know he was sick for a long time and his heart just gave out. But he loved you more than anyone else in the world." Anthony sat silent, unmoving.

Linda and I began to talk about the arrangements that were being made by Grandma and Jeni. They had come to the house earlier so Linda could be involved in planning the ceremony that would take place at Good Shepherd Church on Friday. Linda had asked our next-door neighbors, the Ludys, to keep Alex while we were at the funeral and burial. Gail would take

care of Anthony in our absence. Linda's brothers and wives were scheduling flights and both had planned to stay through the weekend.

We were so focused on details, it was awhile before we noticed Anthony sitting with his head bowed, tears rolling down his face, soaking his lap. This heartbreaking message had somehow reached him, touched him, and made him cry. He knew he had lost his Grandpa, his biggest fan, the man who had idolized him.

We were startled to see this emotion. He couldn't walk or talk, but he could cry. For a third time, we had caught a glimpse of our Anthony. Linda knelt by his chair, comforting him, telling him how much Grandpa loved him, hoping to get a response. But shortly Anthony stopped crying and was gone. The blank face and empty eyes were in place once again.

Grandpa was buried on a wintry Friday afternoon at Gate of Heaven Cemetery. He had a picture of Anthony in his jacket pocket, right next to his heart.

CHAPTER 16

Snow Therapy

FEBRUARY 1999

It was a Saturday in early February. We were in the dining room, wrapping and boxing china from the cherry hutch that we would move to the basement. Only six months ago we had renovated this room. We had refinished the original wide-board and peg wood floors a natural honey color and painted three walls eggshell white. The back wall, which we had painted a burgundy color, framed large windows that looked out over the backyard. In winter we could follow the headlights as they travelled up the long hill of Bluewing Terrace several blocks away. Always the warmest room in the house, we loved to light a fire and eat there during the frigid months. And every Sunday dinner took place in this room.

Several months back Linda hired Earl, a semi-retired carpenter and handyman, to remove the dark colored built-in bookshelves in order to install double French glass doors in the wall leading to the family room. Earl had taken down a seventies-style Mediterranean mantle from the painted white brick hearth, returning a beautifully constructed white work of art as

replacement. He had installed crown moldings and hung a chandelier of twenty-four glass prisms above our cherry dining table and eight chairs.

The colonial-style house, which we had bought from Linda's parents a couple of years before, had been perfect to accommodate us when we had moved in. But now Anthony was in the family room because his second floor bedroom made it impractical to use. Since we needed space on the first floor for therapy, we had decided to sacrifice our dining room. It was big enough to hold the necessary mats, massage table, bench, wedges, therapy balls, and odds and ends. It gave us a place to store Anthony's leg and arm splints, his wheelchair when he wasn't in it and the Hoyer lift that the hospital insisted we keep, even though we refused to use it. There was also a standing oval mirror that we would place in front of Anthony to allow him to see what his body was doing during therapy, a technique we learned at Children's. Victor, the homecare occupational therapy assistant, had built a frame out of plywood and installed it on the long wall facing the fireplace where Anthony, strapped at the knees, hips and chest, stood erect, twice a day, for thirty minutes.

Linda finished boxing the china while I moved the chairs down the stairs. A little while later, Mike, from next door, and his son, Chris, helped me move the table and hutch to the basement for storage. The dining room was now empty except for the large Oriental rug, which we would leave as a cushion for those of us who would be down on hands and knees, working with Anthony. We moved all the equipment that cluttered the family room and the small study, into the new rehab area.

As I surveyed the newly outfitted room, I knew we would miss the warm and comforting dining atmosphere we had cre-

ated here. But Anthony's needs came first and his rehabilitation was our top priority. Our Sunday meals had become less than the leisurely, conversation-filled events that we had been accustomed to and were now more or less disjointed, as Linda was up and down tending to Anthony. We were still feeling the absence of Grandpa and so, while we continued with our weekly tradition, these meals had become perfunctory. We would make do by eating in the kitchen. The lifestyle changes would be worthwhile as long as Anthony's condition improved and he regained his physical abilities.

• • •

On Sunday we woke to a snowstorm. Beautiful, but destructive, the roads and streets were treacherous. Bev, the nurse, lived in Mason, only five to seven miles away, but she was a few hours late while waiting on the hilly streets leading up to our home to be cleared. It was after noon before she was able to care for Anthony.

In the meantime, Alex and Natalie were building a fort in the front yard. They had taken the red recycling bin and were packing large snow bricks inside of it, which they would layer on top of others, constructing the necessary walls of the structure. Their seven and eight-year-old bodies busy, they were focused on this chosen task, at least until something else caught their attention.

As I looked out the window next to Anthony's bed, the girls waved, prompting me to come out and help. I couldn't bring myself to leave Anthony inside while I went out to play with them. Although basketball, and recently fishing, had been Anthony's passions, playing in the snow had always been the

favored activity when a winter storm blanketed the area. Anthony had spent hours building forts and tunnels, sled riding on the nearby golf course and learning to snowboard.

Linda reminded me regularly that we needed to be cognizant of not excluding Anthony. She was always afraid that he would feel left out. The fact that he didn't seem to recognize night from day made no difference. In her mind, Anthony might know, and this was simply unacceptable to her. I understood, even if I didn't agree, that we should do only the things he could do with us. In this case I stayed inside until Jeni arrived.

By then, the girls had the sleds out and were riding down the small hill in the front yard. I decided that I would take Anthony outside as well. No small task, Linda, Jeni and I bundled him up in layers of clothing, put a ski hat on his head and mittens over his spastic hands. We pushed his wheelchair to the front door and the three of us picked him up; Linda and Jeni each took a leg while I carried his upper body. We made our way down the two front steps and placed him in an inflated inner tube that we had pulled behind our run-about at the lake in seasons past. Well seated, his rear in the hole of the tube, he couldn't fall out.

The yard sloped just a little toward the neighbors. Not a big slope, just enough for a sled to glide easily into the adjoining yard. Using the towrope, I pulled Anthony down the small hill. The ride lasted all of three seconds but at the end, as I turned to look at him, I was elated to see he was smiling. Linda took pictures of his snow-covered woolen hat and pink cheeks and the first smile we had seen from our son in months. Linda's sister Jeni watched in amazed delight.

Anthony's reaction motivated me. I hadn't seen him smile

since the day we transferred from Cardiac Care to Rehab and his response gave me hope. Even though his face had again taken on its usual vacant look, he seemed to be doing fine and I was sure he needed to have some fun. The last six months had been anything *but* fun, and formerly he had been like any twelve-year-old boy. He had lived to have fun.

This time, we would change the ride up a little. After loading Anthony in front of me onto a long yellow plastic sled, Linda, Jeni and the girls gave us a shove. Two seconds later we were at the bottom of the hill. My weight and the hard shell of the sled had given us a little more speed and distance. When I looked to see how Anthony was doing, he was grinning ear to ear. We did it again. And again. Each time, it was obvious that Anthony was having a ball. Each time, we all watched his face change from its expressionless mask into one of delight.

I decided to take it up a notch. The girls and I dragged Anthony, who was still lying on the sled, to the back yard. Our backyard was quite a bit bigger than the front, and the slope, from the back screened-in porch to the woods, was forty to fifty yards. But we needed momentum and a steeper slope to get a real ride so I removed the seven-foot slide from our swing set and set it on the top step of the porch, propping the screen door open and out of the way. This impromptu ramp provided a nice solid launch pad, which would help us generate the speed and momentum we needed to go a longer distance.

The girls test-drove the ramp. They were thrilled when the sled took them almost to the woods. We packed snow around the new launch to make sure the transition from slide to ground was smooth and attached a rope to the back of Anthony's sled. I pulled him up the ramp, to inside the porch. Linda and Jeni held the rope while I sat Anthony up and squeezed my six-foot,

four-inch frame onto the four-foot sled behind him. Once I got my legs wrapped around him for stability, they let go and pushed. Down the slope we went, almost to the woods. The ride lasted five to seven seconds. When the sled stopped, we both fell off into a foot of unpacked snow.

This time I was overwhelmed when I saw Anthony's reaction. His whole body was laughing and he seemed fully alive. Even if it was only for a few seconds. He was grinning from ear to ear as if this were the greatest ride in the whole world. And for him, in that day, in that moment, it was. Somewhere in the mangled mass of brain cells I saw my son.

Linda, Jeni and the girls had run down the hill to help. They were all excited at his reaction, laughing and yelling "Let's do it again!" Several more times, we dragged Anthony and the sled up the hill, to the top of the ramp, and rode to the bottom, each time gathering speed as the snow packed tighter.

To say I was exhausted when we got Anthony back into the house was an understatement, but I was also elated. When we took Anthony to Florida we learned that we could take care of our son; that he wouldn't break. We learned to live with people staring at him and at us. We learned that, even if we couldn't "fix" Anthony, we could adapt. That day we figured out how to create joy. The once simple activity of sled riding had brought laughter and smiles to faces that had known nothing but pain and sadness for the past six months.

April 1997
Tony and Anthony at
Opening Day, Cincinnati Reds

Spring 1998
Symphony Concert

Summer 1998
"Fishing is Life"

September 1998
Anthony in the ICU

September 1998
Linda, Tony and
Anthony

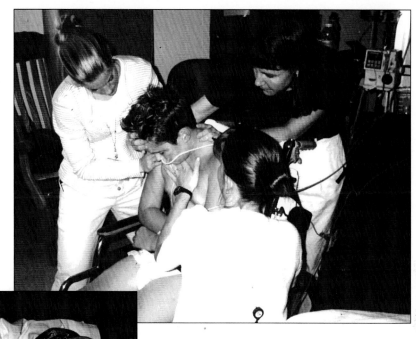

September 1998
First time out of bed

October 1998
Still in a coma, strapped into a wheelchair

October 29, 1998
A moment of
recognition –
"Pig's Legs and
Flapjacks"

November 1998
Third month in a coma,
standing on the "Tilt Table"

November 1998
Home for Thanksgiving

Christmas Eve 1998
Linda and Alex reading
*'Twas the Night Before
Christmas* to Anthony

February 1999
Anthony and Alex
tubing in the snow

August 1999
Anthony's first trip back to
the lake to celebrate his birthday

September 1999
Back to school after one year
out. Anthony with his bus driver
Waldo, Nurse Gary, and Alex

September 8, 1999
Celebrating Anthony's life
at Willie's, with sister
Alex, best friend Nick
and Nick's brother Josh

Winter 2000
A moment of silliness

May 2000
At The Pinnacle Club with a fan

February 1, 2004
Super Bowl Sunday.
Uncle Ray, Tony,
and Anthony

June 1, 2008
High School Graduation
with aide and friend John Traub

Christmas Eve, 2008
Life goes on –
Tony, Anthony,
Alex, Linda,
Pat (Grandma),
Jeni and Steven

July 2009
A rare ride on a Sea-Doo

CHAPTER 17

Training in NYC

MARCH 1999

It was early morning on Monday, March 8 and I was hustling from LaGuardia Airport to USI's New York City headquarters in the cold, grey shadows of the tall buildings. I looked out the window of the dirty cab, watching preoccupied businessmen and women hurry to their offices through the chill. City service workers had blocked off a lane every block or so, it seemed, mostly working above sewers that let off a faint gray trail of smoke, a result of the warm moist subterranean gases meeting the frigid outdoor air.

I loved visiting New York City, summer or winter, fall or spring. From the time I started training here several months prior, I had looked forward to the busy, high-pitched hum of life in this unique metropolis. The constant activity awoke something in me, made me sit up straighter, stand taller, move faster. Knowing I could walk out of the hotel and wander down the street at nearly any time of the day or night and find an open restaurant, store or bakery seemed such a novelty compared to my calm suburban life. The variety of nationalities

and multilingual conversations taking place in this melting pot intrigued me, reminding me that there was a world beyond Ohio.

Someday, I wanted Linda and me to live here. I knew she would love New York City. The ability to walk anywhere and everywhere, the places where families gathered and took pictures, the street vendors, the bright lights and pulsating life of a big city. I had hoped to bring her to New York during the holidays so that we could see the sights together—the Christmas tree at Rockefeller Center, the windows of Macy's Department Store, Mass at St. Patrick's Cathedral, Tiffany's. I had taken them all in alone, but they would be so much richer when shared with her.

Now those plans were on hold. According to the doctors, Anthony's condition would dictate our ability to travel, where we could live, even whether or not we could go out to dinner. I had never liked boundaries. I had always believed that I could do anything I wanted to do, that my ability and desire would overcome any obstacle. I wasn't ready to be limited by Anthony's dependence.

I made up my mind that I would find a way to have this time with her. I didn't know what the future held, but I did know that it had been just the two of us before the kids came. I was determined not to lose every bit of our time together. Maybe we wouldn't live here, but I would convince her to visit someday.

• • •

"I'm here because this organization has decided to go from good to extraordinary and each of you have chosen to do the

same. A few months ago we reviewed your assessments and, based on the results, we know that fifty percent of you are making excuses—the economy, the competition, underwriting. The list goes on. These factors can influence your ability to sell. I'm not going to stand here and tell you otherwise. But ..."

This had been a tough group to work with at first. These proud, professional New York producers had initially been wary of me, less than open to the techniques and ideas I brought to them. So each time I came to town, I went to dinner with one of the salespeople. We would review pending cases, role-play a call, or talk about individual goals and dreams. Over time, several of them had come to trust me and had decided that my sales strategies and techniques had merit. These leaders had smoothed the way for me with the rest of the group. We now had open and often fierce discussions when there was disagreement with my approach.

"The reality is that if you want to buy the bigger house, send your kids to a private school or get that boat you've been thinking about, you need to stop making excuses, set clear goals and be committed to reaching them." My voice changed from instructional to conversational:

"A couple of guys were hiking in the woods. As they walked along, they came upon a bear. One of the guys quickly donned his running shoes. The other, looked at him and asked, "What are you doing? You can't outrun a bear."

The first one replied, "I don't have to. I just have to outrun you.""

After the group stopped chuckling I said, "The point of the story is this—you have to set goals—but not just any goals. The goals must be consistent with where you are and where you really need to be, and you must be committed to reaching them.

Roll up your sleeves. Put on your running shoes. Let's get started."

I worked hard, as I always did, but with more than my usual sense of urgency. I knew that I had to make a difference in sales here or I would be gone. The stakes were higher than they had been just a few months ago. I had to support my family's growing financial needs. My intense personality grew ever more passionate.

• • •

I called home after dinner. Linda answered the phone. She sounded tired. She was curt and distant. She and a nurse had taken Anthony to HBOT in Kettering. It was a long day. Bev arrived at eight a.m., bathed, stretched, fed and dressed Anthony. At ten a.m. she and Linda transferred Anthony into the car and drove to Kettering Hospital, about forty-five minutes away. They undressed him, put him in the mono-chamber for an hour and a half. By one p.m., they had dressed him and transferred him back into his wheelchair and into the car. This was the HBOT schedule every Monday, Wednesday and Friday.

While three sessions per week were less than optimal per the HBOT experts, Anthony had monthly doctor appointments with several different disciplines including neurology, gastroenterology and rehabilitation. Each of the doctors followed Anthony closely, ordering tests and adjusting medications as they felt necessary. Since Anthony also had physical, occupational and speech therapy sessions three times a week, his days were full.

When they got home from the hospital after HBOT,

Anthony would rest for an hour and a half and then be up for therapy from three-thirty to four-thirty. Back in bed for half an hour, the nurse would give him an enema and clean him up after his bowel movement. She would then go home for the night.

After dinner, we would get Anthony out of bed and lay him on the floor to stretch his back and his arms and legs, or have him sit Indian style or with his legs extended out in front. We worked diligently, hoping to help Anthony maintain his flexibility. After stretching, we would get him up from the floor and prop him under each arm while attempting to walk him the few steps to his bed.

Nearly every night Jeni, Linda's sister, came over. While Jeni had always been present in our lives, she had become a daily helper when Anthony went into the hospital. She had been with us from the first critical neurology consultation onward, spending most of her evenings at the hospital tending to Anthony, taking him for walks, bathing him and tucking him in for the night while Linda came home to be with Alex and me.

A career-driven executive at Fifth Third Bank, Jeni worked long hours during the day, then turned nurse, therapist and best friend at night. Her presence provided a much-needed buffer between Linda and me once Anthony had come home from the hospital. We learned to keep our angst to ourselves, knowing we couldn't afford to lose her. These were stress filled, painful times when lashing out would have contributed to our already downward spiraling relationship, and Jeni's presence offered a dynamic that focused our energies away from each other. Needless to say, our family had come to rely on her heavily during the last six months, physically and emotionally.

I turned my attention back to our phone conversation.

"How are things there? Anything new?" I asked. Each time I asked this question, I hoped she would tell me that Anthony had opened his eyes, looked at her and asked what was for dinner. Or that in therapy he had started to walk again. Or that he had tried to get out of bed.

"I had to have the water heater replaced today. I wanted the plumber to install the lift in the bathtub for Anthony, but they were in such a hurry, they couldn't. In fact, they told me to call the office to schedule another call," Linda said irritably.

I wasn't surprised the water heater had died. It was over ten years old. Recently, we had had the thermostat on it replaced, and we had been informed that the water heater probably wouldn't last much longer.

"Okay," I said absently. I had been working on a new training module and didn't want to lose my train of thought.

"How was your day?" Linda asked the usual question, which translated meant 'How is the account progressing?'

"Good. Had a great session today. We're making headway." Being from New Jersey, I felt a certain level of comfort with the strong personalities in the fast paced, edgy New York City office. But it took time to build the necessary credibility that allowed me to affect behaviors.

After a little more chitchat we signed off. Our conversations these days were mostly short and direct. We rarely wandered outside the realm of our immediate needs, mostly because there was nothing positive to talk about since Anthony wasn't improving and everything seemed insignificant by comparison.

Alex was adjusting, with the help of Ms. Landis, the counselor at school, who had arranged to visit with her twice a week. The principal at Blue Ash had given her an unlimited pass to leave class to visit with Ms. Landis anytime she felt the need.

Alex didn't talk a lot about Anthony's "disappearance," probably recognizing how difficult it was for Linda and me. She dealt with his absence in her own way, surrounding herself at night with her stuffed animal collection and a framed photo of Anthony in his football uniform from the prior year. Alex had always been a bright, bubbly personality, and while she had become more subdued in the recent months, she escaped reality with the help of Natalie, playing dress up and pretend nearly every day. They often performed for us, and for Anthony, perhaps hoping he would respond like he had once upon a time.

A little while later my cell phone rang. It was Linda. She had smelled gas in the basement when she had opened the door on her way to do some laundry. She had called the gas and electric company who was sending someone out to check it. She tended to worry a lot, so I didn't think much of it.

At eleven p.m. Linda called to tell me that the serviceman had found several gas leaks on the pipe leading to the water heater that had been installed earlier. He opened the doors and windows to allow fresh air into the basement and informed Linda she was lucky. She and the kids would have been dead by morning. The gas would have permeated the house and the pilot light in the kitchen stove would have caused an explosion. He patched the seeping areas and advised Linda to register a complaint with the plumbing company.

As I listened to Linda recount the story, I wondered what would have happened if she had decided to wait until the next day to do laundry. Would she have noticed the odor before it was too late? Or would I have gotten a phone call telling me my family had perished in a hellish explosion?

CHAPTER 18

Training in New Hampshire

APRIL 1999

I awoke to Linda nudging me. "The weather sirens are going off. Turn on the news," she said.

It was about four-thirty Friday morning and still dark. We could hear rain and far off thunder. We lay in bed looking at the Channel Five weather map on TV. All the local stations were following the same storm system working its way east from Indianapolis toward Cincinnati. We watched dark red and orange colors representing the ominous storm pattern heading in our direction. When we saw our city of Blue Ash come into view, we decided we had better get the kids downstairs.

I awoke Alex while Linda went downstairs and disconnected the feeding tube from the port in Anthony's stomach. A sleepy Alex opened the basement door and turned on the lights. We gathered Anthony up, me carrying his upper body, Linda carrying his legs, and started down the stairs. A door at the bottom led to a small room, the only windowless room of the entire house which served as a toy room for the kids. We put Anthony in a velour armchair in this room that was formerly Grandpa's

study, before Linda's parents had sold the house to us. We told Alex she and Anthony needed to stay inside this room together while Linda and I sat on the sofa just outside, monitoring the storm on TV.

We sat in front of the open sliding glass doors, monitoring the storm. Little did we know that a tornado was nearby and had touched down within two miles of our house. We spent an uneventful hour in the basement, waiting to make sure the dangerous weather was out of our area. Meanwhile, we could hear Alex playing in the toy room, talking to Anthony who seemed, by the look on his face, to be enjoying our little adventure. The news was sketchy at this early time, although it became clear that parts of Blue Ash and Montgomery had been damaged by the storm. Eventually, we carried Anthony back upstairs and settled him into bed.

As the morning wore on, we heard that the deadly tornado had killed four people in our area. An F4 category storm, the intensity of this tornado devastated homes and families. Sycamore Schools closed for the day and several buildings had been turned into shelters for those whose homes were uninhabitable.

I had an appointment with my chiropractor later that day and it was then that I witnessed the devastation firsthand. The landscape near the high school, where the tornado had touched down, was forever changed. Houses were reduced to rubble or had completely disappeared, leaving only cement foundations. Roofs were gone, walls of homes were down, and trees were sheared off as though someone had taken a giant saw to the area. Virtually every tree within a half-mile wide path had been snapped in two.

The stories were all around us; families who had gotten to the basement in the nick of time, a girl whose father rescued

her as she levitated from her bed along with the roof, a baby found amongst the debris unharmed. One lucky driver had landed upside down between two concrete dividers on Interstate 71, his truck wedged neatly between the barriers, leaving the cab intact. Some of the stories weren't so fortunate. A Sycamore High School student lost both of his parents when the winds threw them into a drainage ditch. Two drivers on nearby highways died when the tornado took control of their vehicles.

But we lived. A strange sense of security, however false it might have been, surrounded us. In our minds, we were insulated from the storm and all other bad things because we already had our tragedy. Linda and I knew that God wouldn't let another disaster befall us. Our minds could only accept so much tragedy, thus we shut out the possibility. Obviously tragedies of greater proportion occur around the globe with regularity, we knew that, but somehow we felt we had paid our dues and were immune.

Maybe this illogical reaction was a result of Anthony's tragedy seeming so random, so out-of-the-blue. We had always made sure our kids were in car seats, wore seatbelts and bicycle helmets. Both were good swimmers at a young age because Linda wanted them to be able to save themselves should they fall into a swimming pool or lake. Anthony hadn't been a daredevil. He had been a cautious young child, just learning to enjoy the Vortex at Kings Island amusement park at the age of twelve, when he got sick. He had been known to yell at a speeding neighbor to "slow down" while playing basketball on the driveway. His personality didn't lend itself to dangerous antics and none of the things that we had taken precaution for, or had warned him about, had transpired.

Despite all of our precautions, Anthony had a debilitating brain injury. All the precautions hadn't helped. In the end, an undiagnosed and rare abnormality of his heart, something we didn't know to ask about or prevent, changed his life drastically and permanently. In the end it was out of our hands.

It had become more difficult for me to leave home since Anthony's heart attack. It seemed that every time I went out of town, something went wrong. The first time I left, an ambulance had taken Linda and Anthony to the emergency room. Then her dad had died while I was in New York. A gas leak in the water heater while I was away had scared us both. Linda was trying to juggle office operations, doctor appointments, case managers and the health insurance company. She was managing staff, who sometimes didn't show up and she was tending to Alex. She was solely responsible for Anthony from six in the evening until a nurse showed up at eight the next morning. But neither of us questioned our commitment to our clients or our business and I was on the road once more.

I caught an uneventful flight to New Hampshire except for the strong winds that always rocked the Comair jet upon landing in Manchester. I steeled myself for the usual bounces and wind shear certain to push the jet to the right of the designated runway. Somehow, the pilots and the computers landed us safely.

It had been two years since I first met Tim and began working with him. We had become great friends and shared a common view of business, faith and ethics. We had talked about everything from Yankees baseball to his conversion to Catholicism. As a result of my plane's late arrival, Tim was unable to pick me up at the airport.

I took a cab to the downtown Holiday Inn, home while in

Manchester. I stayed in the same room on the same floor with a view overlooking the square, which served as a gathering place in nice weather. Later that month I might see beautiful flowering trees, but winter hadn't yet given way to spring. The usual cold, cloudy, misty New England weather hung close to the ground.

After dropping my bags off at the hotel, I walked the two blocks to USI's office, thinking about the one-on-one meetings I had scheduled for the morning. My first was with Nate whose new business production had slipped in the past three months. I entered the building through the back door off the parking lot and settled myself in the small conference room. Nate showed up as I turned on my laptop.

"Hi Tony. How is Anthony?" he asked. I had come to expect this question everywhere I went. People always wanted to know, hoping to hear that he was better. Those with children were particularly attuned to the answer. It reminded them of their own vulnerability, I imagined.

"He's doing okay. He's still on a feeding pump, but the speech therapist is teaching him to eat pudding."

Before his heart attack Anthony loved to eat and to tell stories. Linda was sure that if he was motivated to do anything, it would be to use his mouth. Her first goal was to get him eating again. She reasoned that this would restore a fragment of normalcy to his life and maybe facilitate his speaking skills.

Nate and I reviewed his lackluster performance. He admitted he'd lost the motivation that helped him maintain his activity of last year. Even while I coached him up, I doubted that he would be with the company much longer. He no longer possessed the internal desire and commitment that were necessary to enforce tough selling activities like prospecting.

I met with two other salespeople, both of whom were doing well, but could do better. My day had been shortened as a result of a cancellation from Dick, who was off-site working with a client so I made my way to Tim's office down the hall from the conference room. When I told him I was done for the day, he told me to grab my coat. We were going for a ride.

As we got into his car, Tim told me that he had just bought a place in York, Maine, about a half a mile from Nubble Lighthouse. "The Reason," which they had named the house, sat high on a cliff that overlooked the beach and town of York. On a clear day, he told me, one could see the legendary Isles of Shoals and Boon Island Light, a lighthouse that sits on a tiny piece of land famous for the cannibalism that sustained survivors from the wreck of a British ship called *Nottingham Galley*.

Over the next hour and a half, Tim and I discussed the one-on-one sessions I held earlier, the group session scheduled for tomorrow and our individual professional challenges. As usual, Tim asked about Anthony. I gave him the practiced rhetoric that I delivered regularly. As I rambled, Tim stopped me. "Tony, you sound like one of the salespeople as they discuss their prospect pipeline. I appreciate your attempts to stay positive. But this is me you're talking to. Tell me, how is it really going?"

I was silent for a moment. "Well, he isn't making any progress to speak of. Sometimes he seems to be more aware, but he doesn't say or do anything. It's just a look in his eyes. He has no control over any function. It's like his brain has been wiped clean. He doesn't have the capabilities he was born with. He can't scratch when he has an itch—or maybe he doesn't even know he has an itch. He can't suck from a straw, can't rub his eyes, and can't blow his nose. He can't let us know if something is wrong. He just lies there."

Tim asked how Linda and I were holding up. I honestly didn't know. Our lives were awash in nurses, insurance, therapies, doctors, taking care of Alex and myriad mini-crises like gas leaks and flooded kitchen floors.

Tim reminded me to stay focused on Anthony and Alex. That our job as parents was to be there for the family. He encouraged me to read the Bible, to pray and attend church. He reiterated the need for a strong faith.

I was overwhelmed enough already and adding more things to do didn't seem possible. I was doing as much as I could. I was ready for this ride to be over.

Thankfully, we pulled up to "The Reason." The little bungalow sat high off the road. It was small, old-fashioned and in extreme need of a makeover, inside and out. Tim showed me through the house, which took all of five minutes. A large windowed room, which had been added to the back of the cottage, looked out over the shallow backyard that gave way to sky and sea. As we stepped outside the door leading from the house to the yard, I immediately understood what Tim was excited about. The view was remarkable, even for a cloudy, misty Maine day. Off to the west a thumb shaped shoreline formed the beach of York. To the south and east the Atlantic Ocean spread out, the waves of which swelled and crashed on the rocky coast seventy feet below the cliff.

As I took in this awe-inspiring scene, my thoughts turned to Anthony, as they often did these days. Would he ever have the opportunity to experience beauty like this? Would he know the joys of life that I had taken for granted? Would he ever feel the rush of a lover's touch? Would he ever know the comfort and commitment of growing old with a wife? Would he ever have the chance to feel fatherly pride at his own child's accomplishments?

Tim graciously offered to let Linda and I use "The Reason" whenever we wanted. I appreciated his generous gesture, but doubted that Linda would leave Anthony in the care of others anytime soon.

During the group session the next morning, Nate told us, "It's hard to sell insurance, to prospect, to push people for appointments and decisions in this market. Tony, I don't think you understand how hard it is right now."

My no-nonsense personality had become ever less empathetic since September 8.

"Nate, let me tell you about *hard*," I told him. Paraphrasing Pat Reilly when he was coaching the Los Angeles Lakers, I said, "With all due respect, these problems you are talking about— getting people to see you, pushing them to make decisions— they are in the toy department of life. *Hard* is knowing that when I get home my son won't greet me like he used to, with 'Hi, Dad! Wanna play Madden Football?' *Hard* is knowing that he may never say anything again. *Hard* is knowing that he will not graduate high school, have a girlfriend, get married or have a son of his own. Don't tell me I don't know what *hard* is."

I hadn't planned this, hadn't seen it coming. I hadn't raised my voice. The words just tumbled out. Tears ran down my face. Sandy was crying. Nate's shoes had become interesting. Dick sat motionless, staring at me. Nikki searched for a tissue. Tim sat in the back of the room, a look of compassion on his face, perhaps knowing this was inevitable, that it was just a matter of time before I lost my game face and let people know how much I was suffering.

"I used to think my job was hard. Now I know what hard is. Let's take a break," I said.

The lesson, unplanned and unsettling as it was, had merit.

Many of these people had made excuses for not selling, for not meeting their goals. The obstacles they used as excuses were trivial in light of those I faced. Because of my history with this group, they understood me. They knew of Anthony and what had happened. They were all sympathetic. But I knew I had to control my emotions in the future.

As a result of this trip, I made a couple of mental notes. First, there are two components to improvement, will and skill. The Anthony I knew had the will. I was sure that the will he had shown as an athlete was buried deep in his brain, and if it was strong enough, he could overcome his lack of skill.

Second, both Tim and Anthony had to leverage their abilities to reach their goals. Tim must hit the company objectives with the salespeople he had. He couldn't just replace them because he would have most of the same problems with different people. He had to coach his current producers, hold them accountable to sales activities, motivate and inspire them.

Anthony must find, within himself, the desire and commitment that would enable him to overcome his limitations. I resolved to coach him on a deeper, more philosophical level, which I hoped would uncover his desire to be as he had been. I would renew his commitment to the behaviors necessary to reach this goal and I had to do it soon. He had a long way to go, and he had less than a year left before the eighteen-month recovery window the doctors regularly spoke about closed.

When I got home later that evening, Linda ecstatically told me that Anthony had focused for the first time while in the hyperbaric chamber at Kettering. She had been playing *The Sandlot*, one of his favorite movies. Partway through the session she saw him watching the movie, his eyes tracking the characters on the screen. When they got home Grandma had called, and

upon hearing her voice through the receiver Linda held to his ear, Anthony smiled.

I guess I should have been more excited but it's not like he talked or sat up in bed. He only focused his eyes. I guess that was progress. But it wasn't nearly the progress he needed to make.

I told myself that it was a good sign. He was moving in the right direction. Maybe he would start responding soon.

CHAPTER 19

Anthony Gets Excited

MAY 1999

Anthony had been home from the hospital for five months. We had moved his bed from the front of the family room to the back corner where he had more privacy and his bed was no longer visible to anyone who came in the front door or down the stairs. Since he had never looked out the front window, had never been able to focus well enough to do so, we realized our initial reasoning for locating him there was faulty. We decided he might be better off toward the rear, where he wouldn't be disturbed by the comings and goings.

It was evening, about nine o'clock, and I had just returned from training Doug Kreitzberg's group in Philadelphia. As I entered the kitchen from the garage, I saw Linda preparing the formula that fed Anthony, pouring it and his prescriptions for the night, into the Kangaroo bag. She had learned to supply the pump so that the fluid lasted through the night. Otherwise, the alarm would sound and she'd have to perform that routine in the dark, early morning hours.

I walked through the former dining room, now rehab room, which separated the family room from the kitchen, to say hello to Anthony. Since he was homebound, insurance paid for therapists to come to our house, and we were intent on making this time as productive as possible by providing any tools they might need. Anthony spent a good part of each day, broken into increments of an hour at a time, in this room attempting to relearn basic skills that had disappeared with his cardiac arrest and brain injury.

As I entered the room, I said, "Hey, son. What are you watching?" knowing he probably wasn't seeing or hearing what was on the TV screen and wouldn't react. I had asked this question countless times and he had never responded. The ability to focus his eyes, that Linda witnessed while he was in HBOT, seemed to come and go. There were times when he seemed to be closer to the surface, more aware of what was going on around him, but they were sporadic.

He had been disengaged for so long that I had become accustomed to his non-responsiveness. However, this time he surprised me by becoming animated. His eyes wide, his mouth moving without producing a sound, he lifted his head from the pillow to look in my direction. I responded jokingly, "Did you miss me?"

I wasn't sure what was going on. I walked over and put my hand on his head. "Hey there, what's up?" I asked softly. His eyes looked into mine and for the first time since he had gotten sick, I felt a connection, a recognition. A shiver ran through me as we locked eyes.

Several times over the last several months Linda or I had pointed out a change in Anthony, thinking it was significant. Each time the medical professionals told us that his actions were

anatomical, not purposeful. But I was sure his clearly focused eyes were trying to tell me something.

"Linda!" I called. "Come quick!"

She rushed into the room, panicked. Anthony reacted again, opening his mouth, looking in her direction and moving his head.

"Hi, sweetheart," she said to Anthony. She turned to me. "He started doing this yesterday. I'm not sure what it means. But I think it's a good sign."

We didn't know what caused this change, but we were encouraged by his newfound behavior. We made a big deal out of his response each time, conversing with him as though he could talk back. His animated reaction became the norm over the next several days when other family members entered Anthony's room.

It was nearly a week before we finally figured out what was going on. He had begun to recognize who we were.

CHAPTER 20

Fun Looks Different

JUNE 1999

There were times I thought I would never laugh again. A cloud of sadness followed me everywhere. I missed my son. I missed our time. I missed our changing and maturing relationship. I missed my family. I missed what the four of us had been together.

Losing a child is so difficult that it often splinters a family into pieces. You might think this is because of the intense loss of the person that each parent and sibling feels, but it is more complicated. In reality you lose another entity, that of your family dynamic. This dynamic, how we related to one another, changed instantly when Anthony disappeared, forcing each of us to learn another role or be left a family in tatters.

Linda, Alex and I were each reeling from the sudden disappearance of Anthony, while trying to adjust our lives to accommodate the medically fragile shell of a person who had replaced him. Our former relationships with him were gone. The comfortable family we had grown into was gone. Our life prior to September 8, 1998 was gone. Forever.

I envision a circle. I stand in the middle of this circle and around it stand all the people who make up my life, with those closest to me, my wife and my children, Anthony, Alex, and Ashley standing directly in front. As I get older and as I lose one of the people who have played a part in my life, a shadow replaces the form of the person who once stood in this circle. But naturally, as time marches on and I age, more shadows appear as people die or leave me behind.

I never expected that I would lose my son, never expected that this form standing in front of me would turn grey, that he would become a shadow. As one of the most important relationships in my life, Anthony lent substance to my existence. The things I said, the things I did, were all influenced, even if slightly, by my son's presence within me. I define myself, like most people do, by my closest relationships. The loss of this closest of relationships shook me. I thought I would never have the capacity to be happy, to smile, to know joy again.

I had always been a focused and serious person, driven to accomplish my goals. "Goofing around" was not something I typically initiated, even before Anthony got sick. While he and I had many great times together fishing, playing video games and sports, there was always a goal to be met—a fish to be caught or a game to be won. In 1999, I was downcast, worried and in a frenzy to put our lives back on track. Having fun wasn't even on the radar. I had two goals, neither of which was fun: save the business and fix my son.

Anthony had been home for six months and Linda had assembled a homecare staff that was caring, reliable and helpful. Each of Anthony's nurses had become a valued family member.

Homecare professionals have a difficult job in that they may spend many consecutive hours in this personal setting, but are

expected to keep their distance. Over time, as relationships naturally develop, it becomes difficult, maybe impossible, to be removed from the dynamic that naturally occurs in any home or office environment where one spends eight to ten hours a day. Ultimately, each of the members of our initial team—Gail, Bev, Don and Gary—came to be friend and advisor to Linda and me, nurse and companion to Anthony, and older sibling to Alex.

Each of the nurse's personalities came to light and cast a positive glow on our dismal daily existence. Gail's upbeat "get-it-done" attitude and experience in homecare started to rehab Anthony and us. Her attention to Alex's needs at this crucial time helped our daughter feel less alone. Bev's nurturing, holistic thought process and gentle touch relaxed Anthony and each of us. Her calm personality was a balm to our miserable and frenetic state. Gary's joking, attentive personality and stories of his National Guard weekends entertained Anthony and all of us. His good-natured, older brother-like threats to Velcro Alex to the ceiling made her feel she hadn't completely lost her older brother. Don's playful personality and love for fun surfaced and we began to smile occasionally. These nurses brought much more than their knowledge of medicine and dedication to Anthony into our home. They gave from their hearts and we started to heal.

Linda had made a conscious effort to find male nurses and therapists. Anthony's life prior to his heart attack had included many men—friends, coaches and teachers—nearly all who had been initially replaced by female nurses. She felt that Anthony would be more comfortable with a male for personal hygiene reasons, and since the nurses were with him for as much as ten hours a day, he might respond better, perhaps make faster

progress, with someone who shared common interests, like sports.

Neither Gary nor Don were what you would expect in a nurse. Gary was a medic in the National Guard who was dedicated to serving our country. He looked every bit a soldier with his cropped hair. A huge fan of the University of Michigan, he was always in competition with the local Ohio State fans.

At six feet, six inches and 260 pounds, Don looked the epitome of a hulking football player whose personality and heart were as big as he was. Gary and Don were both good nurses, attentive to Anthony's needs and willing to contribute their energies to rehabilitation. Linda evaluated nurses based upon their commitment to Anthony's therapy—as well as their medical experience and input—and both men fit her stringent requirements and more. Both easily moved Anthony from bed to wheelchair to standing frame to floor mat, etc.

When we brought Anthony home from the hospital, he was still in a coma. Most people, educated by TV soap operas and movies, don't fully understand comas. In many cases, a comatose patient doesn't just wake up all better, with the happy family waiting to joke with him as if he just returned from a long vacation. Individuals whose brains have been radically affected usually go through stages, identified as Rancho Levels of Cognitive Functioning, of which there are eight. A person who has experienced a radical assault may never progress through all of the stages, remaining at a low level function indefinitely. Or he may progress through most or all of them.

At Rancho Level I, the individual does not react to any stimulus at all. At Level III the individual will show localized response and may begin to follow a simple direction like "squeeze my hand," but will do so slowly and/or inconsistently. At Level

V, he will still be confused and disoriented, not able to understand what has happened and he may not be able to finish a simple task like brushing his teeth. A person may progress all the way to Level VIII, which means he will have gained back most of his physical abilities. However, high-level functions like reasoning, math and executive planning—the step-by-step process needed to accomplish a goal like that of getting out of bed and to work by 9 a.m.—may still be compromised.

When Anthony first came home from the hospital he was considered a Rancho Level II, beginning to react, but inconsistently, to sounds and noises. He stayed at Level II for several months.

Before long, the nurses' abilities with Anthony became evident. Gail's experience with her close-to-same-age sons gave her insight and an ability to relate. Bev calmed him with her gentle range of his limbs and her soothing massages. Gary constantly challenged Anthony to do something new, make some new effort. Don's intentional goofiness was a breath of fresh air. All four were on a mission to help Anthony improve his abilities and they gave him their undivided attention, talking, joking or singing to him, as they changed his diapers and bathed him. Even though Anthony couldn't verbally respond, over time it became clear that he was listening and loving the attention, the jokes, the songs, the stories and the silly antics.

While at first Anthony was unresponsive, eventually Don found that he could get a chortle out of him by tripping over his own feet or running into something. Sometimes this was an act and sometimes not, but either way, getting Anthony to laugh or smile was a great treat and the vise that held each of us inside began to ease little by little. We all started to breathe a bit, to relax, forgetting our worries and sadness for a moment. I

learned, we all learned, through each of the nurses, how to relate to this new Anthony. In time, I felt a pure and simple joy in making him laugh with many of the same clumsy slapstick antics that I had seen Don perform. I started imitating him.

One early Saturday morning, Linda went to the kitchen to get coffee before Alex's T-ball game. A short time later, I heard her scream frantically and I ran to see what had happened.

"What's wrong?" I asked, as I rushed into the kitchen. Linda pointed at the coffee maker sitting on the counter. Even from where I stood I could see a huge centipede. It was so big that it had prevented the filter basket from lining up properly and water was spilling out all over the counter.

"Dad, what happened?" Alex said, running into the kitchen. By this time Linda had retreated to the bedroom with her planner. I had heard her muttering and caught the words "robo-centipedes" and "realtor" as she left. I assumed this meant she wouldn't cohabitate with this insect, or the family that likely came with it, and she was planning to sell the house.

Alex and I examined the five-inch long bug. I poked at it with a knife where it lay half in and out of the filter.

"It's rubber," I said. It appeared authentic.

I was irritated that our busy morning had turned into a noisy, messy surprise. Apparently, Don had left this little present before going home the previous evening. Since Linda always prepared the coffee before going to bed, he had timed his prank for maximum shock.

A few minutes later, Bev showed up. Once she heard the story, she suggested a retaliatory strike and we agreed that Don had earned it. We laid out our plans and went on to Alex's game.

Don called later that day to talk to Bev, who was Anthony's supervising RN. When Alex answered the phone, she told him

that mom had to go to the hospital to get stitches because she had cut her hand on the shards of the coffee carafe which had broken when she dropped it upon seeing the centipede. She also told him that Dad was really mad because they had to miss the T-ball game in order to take Mom to the hospital.

Don talked to Linda and proceeded to apologize profusely, promising to be there to do everything that she couldn't do because of the cut and stitches. Within hours, he stopped by to investigate the damage he had caused. By this time, Bev had wrapped Linda's hand in gauze, in true medical fashion, leaving no doubt that it had been done by a professional.

Of course, Don had to see the actual cut, so he proceeded to remove the gauze. His ashen face pinched up in concern as he began to see a dark red mark appearing through the last layers of the thin fabric. As a skilled nurse, he recognized that this was a deep wound and he knew he was responsible. There appeared to be a lot of blood soaking through the material.

With the final shreds of white and red gauze in his hand, he stood staring at Linda's exposed hand. Instead of the wound he expected to see, he saw red and black markings of magic marker in her palm.

"Gotcha!"

CHAPTER 21

Tony Builds a Deck

JULY 1999

Three months turned to six months and then to nine months. Still, there had been little change, physical or otherwise in Anthony. I had thought, just a year ago, that he would have finished the seventh grade and his first junior high school baseball season, that he would have been gearing up to play summer basketball, or he would have been learning to water ski.

By now Anthony would have been a B.M.O.C.—Big Man on Campus—on his way to eighth grade. He would have experienced football games and dances. He would have spent time hanging out with friends at the mall or the movies, and he might have had a girlfriend. He would have known some of the newfound freedom that becoming a teenager brought. None of these things had happened. He had missed it all. He had missed all but three days of seventh grade and we weren't sure when or if he would go back to school.

What good would it do? How could he learn or demonstrate that he had absorbed anything? Had he retained any of the knowledge he had accumulated before his heart attack and

brain injury? His ABCs? How to count from one to ten? We had no idea what he knew and didn't know. What grade would he be in? I knew that unless we were able to reach him, to move him out of the place he was in, his future looked dim.

We had bought a trampoline with a safety surround net for Alex's eighth birthday in June. We wanted to make our backyard a place where the neighborhood kids would play so that she had convenient playmates and Anthony could participate, at least visually, in the fun. Alex and Natalie and a gang of four or five, loved to jump and play on the trampoline. It became their meeting place and they would hang out there, on the trampoline bed located beneath the trees, when they weren't running the neighborhood, exploring the nature preserve behind our house or riding the zip-line that Mike had installed for Natalie in their backyard.

This was the stuff of childhood summer—the outdoor play time, the freedom to run and explore, the thrill of staying out after dark catching lightning bugs, playing hide and seek, or sleeping overnight in a tent. I remembered that Anthony and Nick had camped out in the backyard once or twice during the past couple of summers. We had always left the back door unlocked, knowing they would end up on the sofa in the basement before the night was over, having been spooked by the black night or a strange noise.

Anthony's carefree days had been cut short. I told myself that he didn't know that he was missing anything when we sat on the screened-in porch while Alex and her friends played in the backyard.

Linda wasn't convinced. She felt that he knew, on some level, what he was missing and she worked to involve him in activities that a kid would choose. She had enthusiastic

partners in Don and Gary, who both felt that fun and recreation were as natural as breathing to a twelve-year-old. Together, the nurses and Linda had devised play times that were safe and enjoyable for Anthony.

Linda and Don would wheel him to the backyard trampoline and wrestle him through the net opening and onto the bed, where Natalie and Alex would join them. Don would wrap his arms around Anthony's chest, pull him to a stand position and gently bounce him. Anthony would have loved jumping on the trampoline, prior to his heart attack. Now though, his spastic muscle tone interfered. He couldn't bend his knees to absorb the impact of the springy surface, so they spent most of their time lounging on the tramp bed beneath the trees, playing games and hanging out with Alex and Nat.

Occasionally, Linda strapped Anthony's feet into his old roller blades. Don would push his wheelchair down the street while Linda made sure his feet stayed aligned on the pavement. Natalie and Alex skated or biked with the three of them, talking and laughing at Don's silly jokes and tricks. Sometimes they played in the cul-de-sac, using Anthony's wheelchair footrests like feet to push a soccer ball, and sometimes they would help him put a soft sponge-like basketball through a pint-sized Fisher Price basketball hoop. Now and then the neighborhood kids tried to talk to him, but his unresponsiveness soon discouraged their efforts and so he sat on the sidelines with us or one of the nurses.

There hadn't been a lot of time for recreation and since Anthony was unable to use his hands or his feet, any activity was a challenge. We continued to try everything we could to involve him, anything to break the monotony of our days. I wondered if we were doomed to spend the rest of our lives at home, bound

by Anthony's disability and a schedule of therapies, medicines, feedings and bed rest.

Any kind of movement for Anthony was difficult. His muscles were in a state of spasticity. After some investigation, Linda decided we should buy a hot tub to help relax his body and to give him something he could enjoy outside. This meant we had to build a deck on the back of the house.

Somehow, this turned into a controversy, which was posted on the large marker board in the rehab room. Nurses, therapists and visitors were expected to vote. The controversy? Which would you spend seven thousand dollars on—a deck or a boob job? All of the men voted for the boob job, except for one, who wrote on the board, "A deck because I can use it anytime I want."

This type of adult humor was a departure from what our household had known before Anthony got sick. Certainly, we were looking for any way to escape the ever-present, crushing depression that threatened to engulf us. Linda and I welcomed any form of distraction that directed our thoughts and energies to positive places, away from the negative environment, which was all around. We kept ourselves moving, never allowing time to wade into emotionally deep waters from which we might never emerge.

Linda's philosophy was that each of us has a limited amount of time and energy. We could choose to spend these valuable assets positively or negatively. Either way, the time and energy would disappear. Staying afloat, emotionally and mentally, was the common goal for both of us, and even though we approached it differently, we each spent these assets attempting to enhance our tragic situation.

Building the deck presented a positive distraction that

would keep me busy. It would hold a hot tub from which we could all benefit. Linda and I planned the deck with the help of the local lumber supply. After digging the holes and placing the support posts into the ground, Anthony's friend, Nick, came by with his dad, Doug, who reminded me that I needed to cement the footers at the base of the support posts. So together we mixed the concrete and replanted the footers.

While this setback would normally have frustrated me, I found that the time I spent working on the deck project was time I wasn't fretting over the state of Anthony and our difficult lives. This hard physical labor in the heat of the summer wore me out and left me too tired to think about all I had lost. I sensed that Doug also welcomed the distraction. Nick's brother, Josh, had long ago been diagnosed with muscular dystrophy and Doug had his own personal challenges. Together, we were soldiers, sharing a foxhole, combating soul-ravaging enemies that debilitated our sons.

My ordered life had been turned upside down. I was at a frustrating standstill with Anthony. My relationships with Linda and Alex were tense. Alex stayed busy and out of my way with Natalie and her friends. Linda worked with the nurses and therapists feeling that they didn't know Anthony like she did. We were cohabitating. We were tolerating each other. But that was about all.

My daughter, Ashley, was looking forward to her senior year at Newport Central Catholic in Ft. Thomas, and was beginning to plan for college. Undoubtedly, she felt ignored. Our family life had turned into a nightmare.

Were we dysfunctional? Definitely. Was it understandable? Absolutely. Would we make it? Questionable.

After three weeks of planning, building and rebuilding, we

had a great deck, solid enough to hold a hot tub and more. I had somehow managed to keep the flooring square inside the surrounding rail and, as I put in the last board, I found I was only a half-inch off perfect. Not being much of a carpenter, I felt pretty good about the end result. I had finally made progress on something.

I remembered building the wood swing set in our backyard for Anthony's birthday. I had almost finished, needing only to attach the swings, the slide and the fireman's pole when three-year-old Anthony asked me what I was doing. I told him I was building a garage for his tools. Although it didn't look like the garage that housed our cars, he didn't question me. His trust in Dad was complete. He immediately retrieved his plastic lawn-mower and parked it under the wooden platform that led to the slide.

That had been nearly ten years ago. Anthony had been three years old, was mostly potty trained, walked, talked and played. Now, he was almost thirteen and he was unable to do any of those things. He had less going for him now than he did as a tot. He had a long rehabilitation still in front of him to regain even his three-year-old capabilities.

He had always responded to me and to my coaching. I knew that he could perform if I just found the right words, the right strategy and the right tactics. I had to help him discover his mo-tivation to work harder. Thus far, my efforts had yielded no gains, but I would find a way to reach him. Until then, I con-vinced myself I had to stay on him. I couldn't let him get lazy. I had to push him like I had pushed the athletes I had trained as a college football coach.

CHAPTER 22

Anthony Goes Fishing

AUGUST 1999

It was August 4, Anthony's thirteenth birthday. Linda and I had made big plans for the day, knowing it would be a tough twenty-four hours. This occasion reminded us of our joy at his birth and the twelve parties, gifts and cakes that we had for him in the past. Thirteen meant Anthony would be a teenager, an age that marked the beginning of the passage to adulthood. Now it would mean nothing to him. He would experience none of the freedom that a typical thirteen-year-old would. He'd never know the anticipation of life's possibilities.

This was Anthony's first birthday since his heart attack last September. Celebrating this year would be difficult because the child we were accustomed to honoring on this day was gone. But we were determined to be upbeat. We would do our best to make sure that Anthony had a good day. We would avoid the emotional minefield that surrounded us by staying busy.

I wondered where he would be, where we would be, in the years ahead when he turned eighteen. Then twenty-one. And thirty-five. And fifty. While in the hospital, one of the doctors

had commented that Anthony's lifespan would be fairly normal. This meant that we would have him in our home until we could no longer physically care for him. He could well outlive us. Would he ever talk? Would he be able to take steps at all? It was inconceivable that he would be in his current state, unable to communicate, walk or feed himself forever.

Anthony's inability to speak was torture to us, but particularly to Linda. She worried incessantly that he was unable to tell us if he was uncomfortable, hungry or thirsty. He had no way of communicating at all since he didn't even cry like a baby would, to tell us something was wrong. To Linda, being locked inside of one's head had to be the worst kind of torture. She, Sandra Grether, the speech therapist, and the nurses made Anthony's communication their number one priority; he had to regain a way to communicate.

It was ten a.m. and Alex, Don and I were all gathered around Anthony's bed in the family room. We all wore birthday hats and blew noisemakers that rolled out and expanded into multi-color tongues. We sang "Happy Birthday" as Linda presented Anthony with a chocolate cake, his favorite. Alex blew out the candles since he couldn't.

"Congratulations, Anthony. You made it to thirteen. You almost didn't," I said. He looked back at me, seeming to understand. "The good news is that you're still on the right side of the dirt." This was an expression we had used jokingly in the past to remind us that we should be happy just to be alive. Someday we wouldn't be so fortunate.

"Anthony, how about some cake and some mint chocolate chip ice cream?" Linda asked, as she came back from the kitchen carrying a tray with several loaded plates.

Recently, I had read a book in which birthday cake had been

served for breakfast and I had decided that this was a great idea. September 8, 1998 was a regular reminder that we had better celebrate while we could. We weren't guaranteed another day or another hour with the people we loved.

We had been advised not to feed Anthony anything solid because he might choke, but we often fed him small tastes of items he wouldn't have to chew. At this point, he handled ice cream pretty well. Before he had gotten sick, it had been his custom to have a bowl of mint chocolate chip ice cream at bedtime. We had kept up this routine, although on a more conservative scale, from the time he had come home from the hospital. Tom, Anthony's first in-home speech therapist, had worked hard on retraining Anthony to eat, and felt the consistency was thick enough that it wouldn't slip down his throat causing him to choke. Linda had decided that cake fell into this category as well. At least on this day.

While we were committed to keeping Anthony healthy, we were also committed to his quality of life. Cake and ice cream fell into this quality of life category. His favorite foods had been chocolate and chocolate mint ice cream, steak and pizza. We hoped he would eat solid food again someday; meanwhile, we would feed him small portions of the sweet, soft foods that more or less melted in his mouth.

"Anthony, we're going to the lake this afternoon, so we have to get everything done before we leave at three o'clock. Don is going to stay late and help us have a great birthday," Linda said.

We had talked about this trip a week before. We were going to take our run-about, which had been sitting unused in the side yard, to Brookville Lake. Since Anthony's favorite hobby had been fishing, we thought that a trip to the lake would be a

good gift, one that he might enjoy. Perhaps, it would bring back memories of other times. Maybe he would feel as he had just a year ago when the family had spent hours each summer weekend on Caesar's Creek or Brookville Lake.

While we were in the hospital, the therapists and nurses had instructed us to bring familiar items to Anthony that would encourage his memory. Old toys, photos, posters, his favorite t-shirts. Anything we could think of. Anthony had loved to have Vicks VapoRub massaged onto his chest and back, so we had him breathe its distinctive and recognizable eucalyptus scent. We figured the same rule applied to experiences. Anything that might tweak Anthony's memory would be positive and might help to bring him back.

We went about the day, doing our chores and getting ready to leave. Don put Anthony through his usual routine of "bed" bath and morning stretching. After standing in his makeshift stander, Don put him back in bed for an extended rest. Anthony would be sitting for several hours this evening while we travelled and while we were on the lake. He would need to be rested before we left.

I had secured our eighteen-foot boat to the trailer hitch and packed my black SUV with a picnic dinner of sandwiches and chips that we would eat while boating. A small cooler held soft drinks, water and Anthony's nutritional supplement.

We wouldn't feed him anything while we were out. He needed a controlled environment so that he focused all of his attention on swallowing, even something as simple as ice cream. He had developed what the doctors called "a startle reflex" and nearly any unexpected movement or noise would make him flinch and jump. We learned to talk softly to him as we entered the room. We now talked him through nearly everything we

did, so that he knew ahead of time what to expect. While Brookville Lake was fairly calm in the evenings, there was often a random boat or jet-ski that provided distracting noise and turbulence that could startle him. As we drove to the lake, we listened to the radio, talked and pointed to landmarks that Anthony might recognize. He hadn't been in the car much except to visit one of his doctors at Children's Hospital. Because of physical limitations, his outings were limited to rare events at Grandma's or Aunt Jeni's, and other special occasions planned in advance.

In July we had taken him to a baseball game that his former teammates had played at nearby Grooms Field. Being in this familiar setting had made me nostalgic. Watching his peers as they enjoyed their freedom, talking, running, catching, batting and congratulating each other had so depressed me that I decided I wouldn't take him to a game again. Since he hadn't shown any signs of interest or recognition, I figured he didn't care one way or the other.

Baseball games were a part of our old life, one in which Anthony was no longer able to participate. Being at the ball field reminded me of our former carefree existence, which I sorely missed. I didn't need any more reminders of what I had lost, what Anthony had lost. I had no desire to see these other kids, who I had come to know well, play ball and develop into young, productive adults. I didn't want to hear their parents talk about their accomplishments, their shortcomings or their future plans. It was easier to avoid it all.

Our life as a family was different now, too. We had left many people and communities behind as we passed into this new, unknown living arrangement. We no longer shared the commonality of the Black Sox baseball team. We didn't even

share the commonality of having an average teenager. We were so busy trying to keep our world from falling apart, that we had little time to pursue activities outside of the few in which Alex was involved. We no longer had the luxury of hanging around and getting to know people. Our activities took place at home, where Anthony was.

Anthony sat in the front passenger seat next to me, while Linda, Don and Alex sat in back. As we rode, Don told stories of his days in the Army while stationed in Alaska and his forty-day kayak trip down the Ohio River to the Mississippi River and finally to New Orleans. His adventures were exciting and foreign to us, since we had spent only a few hours outside of suburban safety. We were swept up in his fear when he was suddenly caught in the current of a barge and in the eeriness of camping alone overnight on the river bank. His sighting of a black bear, while in the Alaskan outback, was a contrast to our zoo experience, where dangerous animals were separated by metal and engineered landscape.

Soon we were pulling around the loop leading to the launch ramp. I stopped the SUV and removed the canvas mooring cover, storing it in the back of the truck after transferring the cooler, food and towels to the boat. In the meantime, Don was standing Anthony next to the passenger side door. Together, we lifted and carried him to the forward port side of the trailered boat and placed him into the lounge seat of the open bow. This had always been his chosen spot, where he could sit as we accelerated over the lake. Anthony loved watching the water rush toward him, meeting the bow of the boat. He had spent hours in this spot, lounging on the padded seat.

There were times when we could tell, by Anthony's demeanor, that he was content and this was one of those times. He

settled in comfortably, a serene look on his face, like he was welcoming an old friend.

Linda, Alex and Don joined him in the boat before I backed it down the launch. Once it was in far enough to float, I removed the hitch. Linda started the boat engine and backed into the water, heading away from the dock. She swung around to pick me up off the pier after I had parked the trailer. I took over as captain and headed for open water. I drove past the buoy line and turned north out of the public launch area, heading toward the shallow, no-wake zone where fishing, swimming or anchoring were allowed. We only had about three hours, since we would have to head back to town by eight. I was on a mission. We had fish to catch.

It was a little before five when we launched, and the daytime population on the lake was beginning to thin out. Sport boaters, those who ski, tube and jet-ski, churned up the waters of Brookville Lake during the day, particularly on weekends. Since Brookville is a small lake by boating standards, the water was often rough and not much fun to be on, unless you were joining in these activities, in which case, the waves and turbulence were a plus, providing extra thrill.

On this Wednesday evening God was smiling on us, providing perfect weather and perfect water for our first trip of 1999 to the lake, Anthony's birthday present. It was a beautiful, warm late afternoon, with just enough wind to make for comfortable anchoring and soon the water would be calm.

Several fellow boaters were also enjoying the late afternoon and, as is customary, we waved at each other as we passed. Shortly, we found a shallow cove, pulled in and anchored so that we could cast into an area of fallen limbs that would seem to entice underwater inhabitants. A couple of fishermen were

trolling the lake down the shoreline and an occasional boat would pass by. But mostly, we were alone.

There is a special quality to the lake at that time of day, when the sun's angle provides a beautiful light on the trees and the reflection on the water becomes less hard, less true, than in full sunlight. The outline of the leaves and the shadows and crevices of the land abutting the lake become deeper and darker as the sun goes down. The air over the water takes on a golden quality while the setting sunlight turns the lake emerald and the shoreline multiple shades of terrestrial green and brown with shadows of grey, until eventually the lake and land become one. It is the perfect time and place to forget your problems as you are presented with a shifting show of unparalleled natural splendor.

However, we were there to fish, so I set about the task of tying off lures and baiting hooks. In the meantime, Linda distributed sandwiches and drinks while Don educated Alex and Anthony on some of the environment that surrounded us. We had often seen bald eagles flying overhead while on Brookville and egrets were a common sight. We knew to look for these. But Don was an avid hiker, as well as an accomplished boater, and his brain was an encyclopedia of natural facts.

While we ate, we held fishing poles, talked idly and watched our individual bobbers for any sign of a nibble. Don sat in the open bow lounger near Anthony, holding a pole since Anthony's spastic hands prevented him from holding the pole at the proper angle. Linda lounged on the back seat and Alex sat on the padded swim platform next to her. I stood, as I always did, looking for fish, ready to reel in my line and recast should I see a dark shadow swim or jump nearby.

Someday, I would catch a fish on this lake. Although we had been coming here for a couple of years, it hadn't happened

yet. I would half-jokingly tell Linda that I needed a fishing boat. That our run-about was the problem because it didn't allow me to troll quietly without disturbing the water and it didn't get me to where the fish were biting fast enough. She usually reminded me that investing in my fishing pasttime was a write-off without the advantage of a tax deduction, since I lost at least two poles each season and spent hundreds of dollars every year on new rigs and lures that I was sure would end my losing streak. She thought I did a fine job of bolstering the economy and Bass Pro Shops while I fed the fish.

Nonchalantly, Linda said, "I think I have a bite." Don and I both looked over to see her pole bending and quivering.

"Reel it in!" we both yelled at her, excited that we had something on the line.

"How do you do that?" she asked.

Don and I both fell over seats and the cooler trying to get to her before she lost this prize. She happily handed over the fishing pole and moved out of the way while I worked at reeling in the catch. Don scooped a ten-inch long catfish into the net and brought it aboard.

Since Anthony was in the open bow facing forward, he hadn't been able to see the action, so I took the catfish to him.

"Anthony do you believe this? After two years of fishing here, Mom hooks the first fish," I said.

As I showed it to him, his facial expression changed and I thought for a moment that he didn't want the whiskered catch too close. But, after a second, as he held the pose, I recognized that he was doing a "Jimmy Houston." He was kissing the fish! There he was again. I caught a glimpse of my old Anthony. I was amazed that he had remembered because I had all but forgotten this ritual.

On our free weekend mornings, he and I had sat side-by-side and watched Jimmy Houston fishing shows, hoping to learn a new trick that would turn us into great fishermen. We loved to see Jimmy pull in his catches, even though they might be "fish actors," a supply of which was kept for use on days when the real things weren't biting. Like Jimmy, Anthony pretended to kiss each of his fish, surely dreaming of how he might be blessed with a Houston-sized bass. Whenever he landed a fish, he had imitated this famous TV angler, who kissed all his catches before setting them free.

I remembered our last trip to visit my parents in upstate New York. On our way, we had stopped to spend the night at a lodge on Chautauqua Lake. Anthony and I had gotten up at the crack of dawn, grabbed our fishing gear and walked out to the end of the pier. The early morning fog still settled on the lake, but the rising sun provided enough light to see out across the horizon all the way to the Highway 17 Bridge. The water was calm as we baited our hooks and began casting.

I have a photo of Anthony from his first catch of that morning. In it, he stands at the end of the pier, a slight hitch in his hip, rod in left hand, fishing line in the other. On the hook is a tiny pumpkinseed fish that isn't a whole lot bigger than the lure he used. He is wearing shorts, his favorite "Fishing is Life" t-shirt, his treasured Michael Jordan basketball shoes and a backwards baseball cap. The look on his face tells me that he is perfectly content with his catch, that fishing to him meant more than the prize, that he was happy to be doing what he loved. We didn't catch any keepers, but it was one of the best mornings we ever had together.

CHAPTER 23

One Year Later

SEPTEMBER 1999

Linda and I were on our way to a conference at the junior high school to meet with a team of special education teachers, therapists and administrators to plan Anthony's seventh grade curriculum. He was returning as a student with special needs and we had to construct his Individualized Education Plan (I.E.P.), which we had never done before. This approach identified specific educational goals that the team would agree were desirable and attainable. Required by the state, an I.E.P. was constructed to protect the student, to hold the school accountable for the student's education, ensuring that no child was left without direction. I hadn't heard of an I.E.P. I was still trying to get used to the idea of having a special needs child and I was still ignorant of all the services and programs in place that support such children.

Bruce Kramer, the Superintendent of Special Services for Sycamore Schools, had put together a group of people who would work with Anthony, to help restore some of his former abilities. A sympathetic leader, Bruce had become the face of

Sycamore Schools, one that Linda relied upon to guide her through this new and bewildering maze of special needs education.

Anthony's new teacher, Mrs. Dinardo, had come to the house in August to get to know Anthony before the entire class descended upon her. Linda told me that Anthony had responded well to her, engaging her with his eyes. Mrs. Dinardo had commented that he had more to give than he was able to express. She felt that Anthony had potential and she wanted to tap it. Young and energetic, she was looking forward to working with him. Her input confirmed my own conviction, which was that Anthony could recover if the right people pushed the right buttons in his brain.

The physical, occupational and speech therapists from Sycamore Schools had also come to the house and evaluated Anthony's abilities during the past month. They were to present their findings, recommend goals and set up therapy schedules during this meeting.

Bruce had suggested that Anthony start later than the rest of the students so that some of the initial chaos of the beginning school year had subsided. This was a big step for us and we agreed. The smoother the transition, the better it would be for Anthony. He would be going for half days on Mondays, Wednesdays and Fridays, which meant that we had to start readying him for school at 7:30 on those mornings. One of Anthony's nurses would accompany him each school day. They would leave at 10 a.m. and would return by bus at 2:30 p.m.

As we drove into the school parking lot that also serves as a playground, I noted the basketball hoops at the edge of the blacktop. This was where Anthony had collapsed a year earlier. I hadn't realized that we would see the spot where he had had

his heart attack, hadn't prepared for this reminder. I hadn't been to the junior high since he had started seventh grade. But I was familiar with the setting because his junior league football teams had practiced under the lights in the adjacent stadium. In a flash, I was taken back to the evenings he and I had spent there, me standing on the sidelines or assisting Coach Allen when he needed an extra hand. I saw Anthony and me talking through this play or that tackle as we walked to the car after practice. I saw us at the season kick-off, the two of us working together announcing players on the loudspeaker the day before his collapse.

Shake it off. Focus, I told myself, as Linda and I walked into the building.

We were escorted to the conference room, where Bruce greeted us and introduced us to the team of people who would work with Anthony. Like his teacher Mrs. Dinardo, each of the therapists had spent a couple of hours establishing a baseline of Anthony's abilities. After we shook hands and sat down, they delivered their findings.

As if we didn't know these things already, they told us that our previously intelligent and athletic son was unable to speak, was disoriented, had no use of his limbs, and couldn't follow a conversation or communicate at all. Since an I.E.P. is designed to set goals based upon currently evaluated abilities which must be openly and clearly identified, we had to hear all of this and agree upon the stated goals.

We had gotten used to Anthony's limitations while at home. It was only when we went outside of our adjusted homebound lifestyle that we would be reminded of his oddness, of his in-abilities. This verbalization of his fully dependent state was a slap in the face. I wasn't prepared for it.

As I sat there listening, a buzzing began in my head. I had to be told, in agonizing detail, about all of Anthony's short-comings. The noise in my head continued to grow as I remembered the aspirations I had had for my son—as an athlete, as a musician, as a student. My ignorance allowed me to think that he would recover from his heart attack and pick up where he had left off. My always assertive nature told me that I would make him normal again.

But as each person reported the devastating information, I recognized that Anthony would never lead a normal life. He would never be an athlete or a musician or a regular kid. He would never again know a normal classroom, or sit in the cafeteria and have casual conversations with friends. He would never play basketball at recess. While they didn't say it aloud, these experts told me that they did not believe he would ever regain his abilities.

They were no different than the doctors who told me that Anthony would never be an independent adult. I was surrounded by people who could not restore my son because their attitudes said this was an impossible task. It *would* be an impossible task if I was the only one who believed that Anthony would recover. I was furious and I made this very clear to the group. I stood up.

"Excuse me," I said vehemently. "Anthony is *going* to recover and I need a team of people who believe this. If you don't, he has no chance. If you are not committed to this specific objective, you are the wrong person for this team. We must all share a common goal of full recovery."

After a few seconds of uncomfortable silence, Mrs. Asher, the occupational therapist spoke. "Mr. Cole, we will all work hard to help Anthony recover, but in the end, it will be up to

him. However, we understand your feelings and appreciate your goal."

She spoke politely, but sympathetically, for the group. I sensed that she was placating me, tolerating me. She was playing the part of a diplomat. I imagined that these meetings, where parents were reminded of their children's shortcomings were never pleasant and ours was one of many in which she regularly participated.

After the meeting, Linda cried as I sat beside her in the car. We had been reminded, once again, of all that we had lost in the past year. I wondered if this would be a forever occurrence. It seemed as though each time I grew accustomed to one dimension of pain, another one appeared. I thought it would never end. I knew that as life unfolded around Anthony, as his former friends went on to high school, I would weep. As they graduated and moved on to college, I would weep. As they married and had children, I would weep.

For these events and all the others I couldn't anticipate, I would put on my game face, but in my soul, I would weep. I would weep for me, for our former family, for the boy I had lost, for the son he had been, and for the adult he would have become. Mostly, I would weep for him, for the life that had once spread out before him, promising college and professional achievement, love and family, travel and faraway places. I would weep for his life that had vanished in a heartbeat.

What was I thinking? I couldn't think this way! If I did, it meant I was giving up. If I thought this way, I was acknowledging that Anthony's state was permanent and I couldn't accept that. I was *not* giving up. I was sure Anthony could regain his ability to walk and to eat and to talk. I knew my son and he

had had the spirit of a champion. He would want more and he would work hard to get it. He would be alright. We would keep working at it and God would help us. Anthony would come back to me. I was sure of it. I couldn't let the naysayers drag me with them. Anthony's quality of life depended upon me.

. . .

Wednesday, September 8, was Anthony's one-year anniversary. A year ago he had been airlifted from the junior high playground to Children's Hospital. Linda and I had decided that we would celebrate this day. After all, Anthony had survived. We were not visiting his gravesite. He had beaten the odds and we were determined to find joy in this. Statistics told us that he might well have died that day, that children's hearts weren't typically strong enough to weather severe cardiac arrest. But Anthony was still with us. Changed, certainly, but with us, and we still had hopes that he would be okay.

Late that morning, after Anthony had worked through his routine of stretching and standing, Gary, his nurse, and I loaded him into the mini-van and took him to the junior high school playground. Gary transferred him out of the car, which I had parked next to one of the basketball goals.

"Anthony, a year ago today you were walking on to this court to play basketball. Do you remember?" I asked him. He looked at me, his enlarged pupils darkening his eyes. I wondered how much he understood.

"You had a heart attack right here. The janitor and the school nurse performed CPR, but you were without oxygen for a while." No response. "You could have died, but you didn't. You fought to stay alive. We're here to commemorate this day,

the day you survived. We're here together to shoot a basket in your honor."

We were about six feet from the basket. I stood behind Anthony, my arms under his, balancing his weight. As I braced his body with mine, Gary placed the basketball in my hands because the spasticity in Anthony's prevented him from opening his palms, from bringing the ball close. I snapped my wrist to send the ball and we all watched as it bounced on the front of the rim, hit the backboard and then dropped through the net. I hugged Anthony, celebrating our two-point accomplishment.

After loading Anthony into the car, we drove to the City of Montgomery's municipal building to see Rob Lantman, the EMT who had stayed in touch over the past year. Every now and then Rob would stop by to say "hi" and to see how Anthony was doing. As luck would have it, Rob was on duty. He introduced us to the rest of the staff, many of whom were familiar with Anthony's story. I thanked Rob and the rest of the emergency staff, for helping to save his life. Then it was time for Anthony to rest, so we headed home.

That night we celebrated Anthony's life, with Jeni and Nick and his family at Willie's Restaurant and Sports Bar. We fed Anthony small bites of mashed potatoes and ice cream, since he wasn't quite ready to eat his favorite meal of Buffalo wings. The waiters sang "Happy Anniversary" to him and we all toasted his survival.

There were moments when Anthony seemed engaged and moments when he seemed to vanish entirely. That night he seemed to come and go as he had many times in the recent past. But we knew he was celebrating when he raised his arms in the air for a toast to his survival. Clearly, he was happy to be alive and with people he loved.

CHAPTER 24

A Better Halloween

OCTOBER 1999

It was Sunday, October 24, and I was on my way to the airport. I was flying to New Hampshire that afternoon for a training session. Since I was going on to Philadelphia from there, I would be out of town most of the week.

As I drove to the airport, I became aware of the bright fall day that was all around me. Good weather to fly. Always a plus. As much as I had flown in the past five years, you would think by now that I would be comfortable in the air, but this just wasn't the case. I had always felt uneasy, particularly during the take-offs and landings, and I had established simple habits that calmed me as I prepared to board a flight.

Some of these habits were good organizational activities that placed my I.D. in the same spot when I travelled. Others, like standing in line to buy a bacon cheeseburger from McDonald's in Terminal C, saved me from experiencing hunger pangs. At least that's what I told myself. But there were some habits, like talking to Linda just before take-off that would unnerve me if I didn't do them and I thought the plane was more apt to crash

if I didn't follow my usual patterns. I had come to recognize that these activities may be rooted in superstition. But I told myself that I was like the pitcher who wore the same undershirt for each baseball game. Everyone has their fears and each deals with them in their way. My habits were my way of coping with my fear of flying.

I pulled into the parking garage and found a spot. Since it was early in the week for business travel, there were plenty of spaces near the Delta terminal. By the next day, this garage would be full and one would have to park way over in the B lot. A spot close to the Delta departure terminal was a perk when leaving town on Sundays, and since my home life was less than perfect these days, I was happy to be travelling early.

I was sure that Linda was relieved that I was gone. While our goals for Anthony were the same, our treatment of him and our approach to his therapy were quite dissimilar. Our parenting styles had always been different, but since Anthony had gotten sick, these differences had become major obstacles. We differed in our expectations and treatment of Anthony. We differed in how we treated Alex, as well.

We fought regularly now, after everyone had gone home. Mostly, we fought about my expectations and interactions with Anthony, although our antagonism seemed to extend to all segments of our lives. Linda felt that I was way over the line in my directives during therapy and she was not shy about voicing her opinion.

But I knew that Anthony was holding out on me. I knew him well, had coached him for eight years, and had parented him for twelve. I knew he could be lazy. I knew he didn't always give one hundred percent. Sometimes I had had to push him. So, I continued to push him.

Regularly, I told him he was not working hard enough, that he needed to stop being a wimp. Since my hard-core coaching methods had worked with him before, they were still appropriate. In fact, when they didn't work, I turned them up a notch, pressuring him even more. I was loud. I was in his face. I was relentless.

Linda had never coached college athletes like I had. She didn't know that I had motivated others to perform in this manner. She didn't know that I had relied on these high pressure tactics to motivate myself to perform. She didn't know what it took to build a winning football team. But I did.

That meant that the team of nurses, therapists, Linda, and even Alex, had to do their part to help Anthony move forward. I expected each to know what was expected of them and to follow through in their assignments. I expected Gail, Bev, Gary and Don to exercise and stimulate Anthony at two to three hour intervals throughout the day. While this was a challenge, given Anthony's need for bed rest, feedings and bowel program, it wasn't impossible. The staff knew that the window for optimal recovery was eighteen to twenty-four months, and we were in the thirteenth month. We were more than half way through this window and Anthony had not progressed far at all. The pressure was on.

Alex had had to grow up in the last year. I now expected her to do her homework, keep her room clean and put herself to bed at night. She had had her mom's assistance for these activities in the past, but since the nurses left at six p.m., Linda had full care of Anthony for the following fourteen hours and wasn't as available to Alex as she had been. Alex knew that she had to pitch in and do her part and she seemed to be handling her responsibilities well. She was doing fine in school and she wasn't demonstrating any emotional problems.

After ten months of Anthony at home, I knew that things ran smoothly while I was gone. I knew I wasn't needed, that things were actually calmer when I was gone. Since this had always been the case, I wasn't insulted. The kids had often asked Linda, "When is Dad leaving again?" after I had been home for a while, the implication being that life was more peaceful when I wasn't around.

Since Linda's dad had travelled regularly, she had grown up in a household that was run by an independent mother and an often absent father. She considered my travel normal, some of it desirable. She believed in the adage, "Absence makes the heart grow fonder." My travel gave both of us needed space and time.

She still felt this way, even after Anthony had gotten sick, and so I felt no guilt as I looked forward to the quiet of downtown Manchester on a Sunday night. I looked forward to the predictable schedule and unemotional interactions of the days that would follow. Travelling and training were balms that now soothed the raw emotions that plagued me at home. I looked forward to escaping the internal turmoil being home provoked.

This arrangement worked well for both of us. It allowed me to focus on business. I was feeling tremendous financial pressure and I knew I had to keep our paying clients. While Medicaid covered Anthony's medical and nursing needs after he had come home, we had recently begun to receive bills from Children's Hospital. Our insurance company was refusing to pay Anthony's astronomical hospital bills.

This didn't come as a complete surprise to us, since Linda's brother Bob was an attorney who had predicted as much when he came to visit in November. But it was just one more obstacle; one more worry to add to the list that already overwhelmed us. Linda had located and retained an attorney, Robert Perez,

who had experience in this area, to sue Golden Rule Insurance. But at this early date, we had no idea of the outcome. I wondered if we would be paying the quarter of a million dollars owed to Children's for the rest of our lives.

In our very first conference, the chief neurologist had advised us that Anthony would likely be dependent and I wondered what this meant for us financially. I knew that the burden of our financial future and his care rested squarely on my shoulders. I had no idea how much money we needed to support him properly if he didn't recover enough to care for himself.

Linda and I had worked hard to get Anthony Cole Training off the ground and had begun putting money into our SEPs a couple of years earlier. Now I wondered how we would ever accumulate enough funds to allow us to retire. I had been working since I was five years old, when I picked blueberries full time. While at age forty-four I wasn't yet close to retirement, I knew that someday I would be tired. I had worked thirty-nine years already. I had looked forward to a time when Linda and I would have some freedom, when we could travel and spend time together. Now, I didn't know what that looked like. Would we ever be able to retire? Would we always have Anthony with us? Would our lives be dictated by his care?

It was dangerous for me to look too far ahead. I wondered where my son would be when I was sixty. I wondered if the doctors were right. I wondered if I would be putting my thirty-year-old son to bed, brushing his teeth, changing his diaper, attaching a urinary catheter to his penis.

• • •

I was in New England during "leaf peeper" season, a beautiful time of year when the plentiful native sugar maples turn bright red, adding a dimension to the kaleidoscope of fall color that I didn't see in the Midwest. The thicket of dark green pines lining the highway on the way to the airport contrasted with the orange, yellow and red of the deciduous trees, enhancing the spectrum of colors. I understood why people travelled from all over to "leaf peep" here. I understood why cars lined the township roads of Maine and New Hampshire to the chagrin of the natives.

I hoped that next year Linda and I could come out here together. We needed to get away from home, away from Anthony and nurses and therapy. We needed to focus on our relationship. I resolved to work on this project immediately. During this latest trip, Tim had offered "The Reason" to us and I would see if we might take advantage of his new get-away after a training session next October.

Tim and I had met for our usual dinner at C.R. Sparks after the previous day's training. Many on his sales team were progressing nicely, although Nate had finally left to pursue his passion in photography. A good move for Nate and for the agency, this would allow Tim to further direct his energies to those who wanted to improve their numbers.

The taxi dropped me at the Delta terminal of the small Manchester airport. I was on my way to Philadelphia and had some time to kill so I ate my usual bowl of clam chowder at the Captain's Galley, then browsed the books in the gift store. As I walked toward the register with a best-selling thriller, I caught sight of the W.W.J.D. paraphernalia displayed on one of the store kiosks.

A couple of years ago, I had been given a W.W.J.D.—

What Would Jesus Do—bracelet by a friend. The concept of the bracelet was to remind one to think through words and actions prior to acting on them. Each time a client or a friend asked me about mine, I unbuckled the clasp and gave it to him. I had given one to Anthony a few months before he had gotten sick and he had followed my tradition, handing his off whenever someone had asked about it. I chose several, in different colors, and one more to replace the last one Anthony had given away.

I wanted something special for Alex. Something that would remind her that I was thinking of her. Something that would tell her that I knew she might be sad or scared. Something that would tell her that everything would be alright. I spotted a silver ring with a thin band and a small amber colored stone. She would know, each time she looked at it, that like the moon, I watched over her. That even if I was out of town, I was thinking of her, that I loved her. Then and always.

• • •

It was Saturday morning and the next day was Halloween. I had decided during the flight from Philadelphia that I had to do something to brighten our Halloween. I couldn't stand the thought of another depressing holiday. I was going to build a Chain Saw Massacre character, dress him in black and position him on the walk leading to the front door of our house.

I worked all day cutting plywood and bolting the pieces together. Finally I had a six-foot form and base upon which to stand it. I took it outside and positioned the figure next to the front porch, tied on a black cape and secured a hockey mask to the face. I attached my electric saw, minus blade, to the

would-be hands of the mannequin and ran an extension cord to it through the window.

When Don arrived for his shift Sunday morning, I was waiting behind the curtain inside, ready for a test run. As he walked up the pavement, I could see him looking curiously at the black form. As he got up next to it, he bent over to take a closer look. I plugged in the cord. The saw came to life and so did Don. He jumped several inches into the air, scrambled backward and cursed.

That was a way better Halloween.

CHAPTER 25

Linda Challenges Me

NOVEMBER 1999

It was the Friday morning after Thanksgiving and I was sitting in my study creating a new presentation when my cell phone rang.

It was Tim thanking me for the gift basket we sent each year. Tim's quiet and unhurried delivery always got my attention.

"I appreciate your business and your friendship," I said. "How was your Thanksgiving?" I asked.

"It was great. All three kids came home from school. I had forgotten how nice it was to have them all here," he said.

I pictured Tim, Eileen and their three college age kids sitting around the table in their warm New England dining room, looking at the snow covered backyard through the floor-to-ceiling window. I imagined the easy conversation, punctuated by frequent laughter that only those who have lived together through life's ups and downs, are able to produce effortlessly; I wondered if our family would ever look like that.

"How was yours?" Tim asked.

"Different. But a lot better than last year. Linda and I ran the Thanksgiving Day Run."

It had been Linda's first organized race and I was not sure she'd do it again. She didn't understand why people would get up at the crack of dawn, drive twenty minutes to the race site and search for parking, to run with eight thousand other people. For her, running was an escape from the constant presence of other people, and the ability to walk out the front door at whatever time was convenient, made it the perfect exercise.

"We came home, soaked in the hot tub for awhile. Then had brunch with the kids, and Linda's mom and sister," I said.

This was the first holiday season after Linda's dad had passed away and we all felt the void of his and Anthony's absences. She was determined to make the holidays different this year and it had been her idea to do the Thanksgiving Day Run.

In the past, we had taken the family on vacation over Thanksgiving. Two years prior, the four of us had gone to Galveston Island where we played putt-putt, fished off the pier, and explored Port Bolivar Island. The kids were fascinated when we drove our rental car onto the ferry that shuttled us between the two islands.

In my study hangs a series of four framed photos of Alex and Anthony from this trip. In each casual pose, a blond Anthony smiles easily at the camera while his arm is slung around Alex, who is missing a front tooth. The colors of Anthony's favorite green Sycamore football jacket, Alex's purple warm-up pants and hot pink jacket contrast with the backdrops of the ocean and a field dotted with yellow dandelions. They look so much younger, even though it was only two years ago.

The Thanksgiving before that we took the kids to Kissimmee, and stayed in a beautiful, new condominium that looked out over one of the canals that dominate Florida residential developments. Every morning Anthony would wait impatiently

for me before going down to fish off the banks where posted signs warned of alligators. We went to The Magic Kingdom at Disney World and Universal Studios and the kids swam in the outdoor pool every night, even though the November air was cool. The year before that we drove to Atlantic Beach, North Carolina, where we had the beach virtually to ourselves.

Life was easier then. The four of us vacationing together was a thing of the past. We had learned when we took Anthony to HBOT in Boca Raton that travelling was too difficult, cumbersome and exhausting. Travelling with Anthony was definitely not a vacation.

Tim and I made an appointment to talk business the following week. I knew he wanted to spend time with his kids while they were there and I didn't want to keep him from that. I was warmed by his thoughtfulness. He didn't call just to thank me for the basket. He called to see how I was doing. It helped to know that he was there if I needed him.

Linda must have heard me get off the phone because she came in and sat down. Sometimes, I didn't mind this distraction. Sometimes, I needed a break and welcomed the interruption. But at other times, I found it annoying that she assumed her presence was welcomed. Those times had become more frequent recently.

"We need to talk," she said.

"About what?" I asked, testily.

I was reluctant to get involved in any conversation with her these days. Our discussions were usually unpleasant and dealt with some aspect of Anthony's condition—medical bills, insurance, a no-show nurse, an endless list of to-do's.

"Business," she said. "Actually the lack of business. Are you ever going to sell again?" Linda handled all operations and

financial aspects of our little company. Her business acumen and degree complemented my education background. We made a good team.

Linda never beat around the bush. She wasted no time letting me know where our conversations were going. She reminded me that we had lost three branches of Acordia when they went through a change of ownership and I had not replaced the business. "We've lost nearly a third of our income in the past sixteen months," she told me, as if I didn't know this already.

Our little company had done well from the start, growing quickly during its first five years. Our clients usually stayed with us for years, proof that our training actually did "drive consistent and predictable sales growth." However, there were happenings that I couldn't affect, like a change in ownership, in which case the new entity often made big changes in personnel and in outsources, like training.

I sat there for a moment letting the steam build, getting ready to explode. "I've been working on new materials. Each year I have to create new modules so that we can keep our current clients. I can't regurgitate the same stuff year after year. I haven't had time to prospect. Get off my back," I said.

"You've become a trainer," she said. She knew this was an insult. She knew this would get my attention.

"You want my job? Take it. *You* get on airplanes. *You* get stranded in airports for hours. *You* get up at the crack of dawn in the dead of winter and walk down sidewalks that haven't been cleaned of snow. *You* work all day and then go back to a little hotel room all by yourself and wonder what the hell has happened to your life. Go ahead, take my job. I'm doing the best I can to keep what we have and you come in here to ask me if I'm

going to sell again. I don't have to listen to this. Get out of my office!"

By this time, she was angry too, and came right back at me. "So, you think being here is easy? You think taking care of Anthony twenty-four hours a day is easier than going out to dinner and staying in nice, quiet hotels? Let me help you with this. The reason you travel all the time is to get away from it all. You can't handle it!" She stormed out of the room.

Twenty minutes later, as I sat in my office, I recognized that she was right. I had lost my focus relative to selling. I had forgotten the great advice that Mike Ludy had given me about not losing the business. Then, I had been cocksure in my ability to stay the course. I even remembered thinking derisively, "There's no way that will happen to me."

But, as I reviewed the past sixteen months, I knew I had been making excuses. I had been telling myself I had to focus on keeping current clients by creating new materials and perfecting existing modules. I had been avoiding the real job of prospecting while I became expert in programs like Excel and Power-Point.

I realized, with a shock, that I was just like the salespeople I coached. I was doing whatever I could to avoid my real job, the job of selling.

My fixation on bringing Anthony back, my depression over losing him, had taken me sideways. Unconsciously, I had lost track of selling while I kept busy with easy tasks. I had given myself a pass on the tough behaviors of prospecting as I wallowed in the depths of my loss. And I was ignoring the advice I was giving every one of my clients.

I knew I had to get back on track. I knew that our current clients would eventually disappear, and if I didn't have new

business to replace them, Anthony Cole Training would be gone. I couldn't afford to lose the business. It would place a strain on Linda's and my already tenuous relationship.

I made a list of people to call, prospects and clients who could refer me to companies who might need our services. I would call them on Monday.

Then I went to find Linda, who was in the kitchen doing the dishes. I put my arms around her from behind and buried my face in her hair. I felt her body tremble and knew she was crying. As I breathed in her scent, I knew that as difficult as my life was, I was sure I couldn't live without her. She was my world.

Years ago, after one of our very first fights, she had jokingly coached me on how to avoid all conflicts by uttering three simple sentences, which I whispered in her ear. "You were right. I was wrong. I'll never do it again."

A couple of seconds later, she pushed me away and turned around. She looked up at me tearfully and grinned. "Well, are you going to sell again or what?"

CHAPTER 26

Anthony Sees Santa

DECEMBER 1999

The holidays had always been my favorite time of year. I had reveled in the music, the hustle and bustle, the glitter and lights. I had forever looked forward to this commercial, overblown holiday, which always provided a welcome distraction from the cold dead of the winter months in Ohio, or in New Jersey where I grew up.

Every year I looked forward to Thanksgiving as the kick-off to the festivities when we had our annual viewing of National Lampoon's "Christmas Vacation" starring Chevy Chase. Each year, Sparky's overly zealous character inspired me to make ours the best-dressed house on the street. My holiday decorating fervor long ago earned me his same nickname, which I am happy to perpetuate.

I had always been enthusiastic about decorating for Christmas, stringing hundreds of lights on our house and landscape and adorning each vertical surface inside with some sort of yuletide knick-knack. As I traveled or shopped, I couldn't refrain from adding to this growing collection and each year, I found a place for even the oldest and humblest of pieces.

My Christmas music collection included nearly a hundred CDs from a variety of genres, from "The Nutcracker" classic symphony to The Irish Tenors' "We Three Kings" to Nat King Cole's Christmas Favorites to The Tractors' "Have a Tractor Christmas." I listened to each of these CDs, playing them constantly from Thanksgiving through New Year's, and I tuned my car radio to this seasonal music assortment wherever I drove.

In the past Anthony had helped me decorate the house, retrieving cartons from the basement, unpacking each ornament and checking each strand of lights. Like me, he had enjoyed the traditions of Christmas, even if he hadn't enjoyed the tedious tasks of untangling and testing the masses of little lights we put up each year.

This had been our normal routine until last year when Anthony was newly released from the hospital. Then, we were at the height of our crisis and the holidays were a blur. I remembered getting the tree up, but that was about all. I was overcome, as we all were, with Anthony's physical condition and our drastically changed lives to pay much attention to the frivolity of decorating. But I wanted to make this year's Christmas better than the last.

It would be a challenge since Anthony was only two months away from the end of the suggested eighteen-month window for recovery and he hadn't made any consistent progress to date. Linda's dad, who had been a big presence in our lives, was also gone. Since Linda's brothers and families were scheduled to come in on the twenty-sixth, we were left with Christmas Eve and Christmas Day to fill.

This was also the time of year when I got homesick, nostalgic for my own family and traditions that were so different from those Linda and I shared. When I was living at home, my

mom supplied a bottomless pot of red sauce and homemade ravioli for the friends and neighbors who would stop by the week between Christmas Eve and New Year's Day. We would sit and talk, play music and sing. For hours we visited, just enjoying each other's company.

My parents had cultivated good friendships to replace their families who lived far away in upstate New York, and they were open and welcoming of everyone. They were simple people who were accepting of all, clearly preferring the presence of others to being alone. They didn't have a lot of money, but neither did anyone else and the presents exchanged were of time and friendship, the most precious of gifts. Those holiday seasons stood out in my mind as some of the best, happiest times, of my life.

• • •

I was in New York City to work with USI for the last time that year. It was always fun to visit in December. The city was dressed in her holiday finery. Store windows and shop displays were bright and glittering. The atmosphere on the street and in the office was more fun, less serious. People were busy making plans and attending parties. Everyone seemed more agreeable. In keeping with the spirit of the season, I typically incorporated games in my training sessions that were tied to a pool of money. Teams of salespeople would vie for the pool, which was eventually donated to a favorite chosen charity.

The New York office hosted an annual holiday party, an incredible event that was being held at the Ambassador Hotel in mid-town Manhattan that year. Jim Butler, CEO of the NYC office, had invited me in the past, but that year we had scheduled training so that I would be in town to attend.

Almost immediately upon my arrival at the party, I ran into Dave Eslick, CEO of USI, who asked me about Anthony. Even though it had been well over a year since he had gotten sick, people always wanted to know how he was. Then how I was. His condition and my state of mind were always linked in that initial conversation. I figured this sequence of questions was because each of them was a parent who had imagined how they would feel in the same scenario. But it might also have been a way to refocus the conversation when I related Anthony's current condition. Everyone was looking for good news, which I wasn't able to deliver truthfully. *"About the same,"* wasn't what people wanted to hear, so they naturally changed the direction of the conversation. It was fine. In fact, it was good. I found it depressing to talk about Anthony's lack of progress all the time.

Sandra Useleman, Senior VP of Training and Development, joined our conversation and, giving me a hug, asked about Anthony. Sandra was also from Cincinnati and she, along with her husband Kevin, had had us to their home more than once. Most recently, all four of us had attended a big pumpkin carving event at her house in October. It was one of a limited number of outings that we had gone on since Anthony had become disabled. We had found it was easier to stay home than to transfer Anthony to and from the car, take on and off his coat, and maneuver his wheelchair up and down the inevitable stairs and stoops.

As our conversation turned to business, Sandra asked if Anthony Cole Training would sponsor breakfast at the annual producer conference as we had done in the past. I assured her that we would and then, to my surprise, she asked if I would speak at the event. This was unusual, since I already had a lot of exposure to their salespeople and USI normally wanted a

different face, a different voice in front of their top producers at the annual Pinnacle Club meeting.

Sandra told me she was looking for something inspirational though, something more motivational than instructional. While I loved giving this type of presentation, my training was more of an instructional, here's-how-you-do-it nature. But I loved getting people fired up because I got fired up right along with them.

I must have had too much to drink by that time, because I suggested that Anthony and I speak together at the session. I had just gotten done telling Sandra that Anthony couldn't talk, couldn't do anything at all, so I was surprised when she quickly expressed her enthusiasm for the idea. She said she needed to run it by Dave, but she was pretty sure that he would see value in this presentation of overcoming adversity. In the meantime, she asked me to hold the date of May 13 for Pinnacle Club 2000 in Boca Raton.

I left the party early to call Linda and tell her the news. I was excited until she said, "Hello. Is anybody home? Do you have any idea of what's involved in carrying this off? It isn't just packing a suitcase and hopping on a plane. This is a huge endeavor. This means figuring out the logistics, the medical equipment, nursing and all the little details that go along with Anthony and traveling. You just don't get it, do you?"

Suddenly, I knew that I didn't get it. I didn't deal with Anthony's specific needs. I had no idea of his medications or his schedule of fluids and nutritional supplements. I didn't know what supplies were ordered or when he saw which therapist or doctor. I was so far removed from their daily lives that I had no idea of what Linda dealt with each hour of every day.

My excitement for Pinnacle Club died, my enthusiasm for

the holidays dissipated. I looked out the window of my hotel room and wondered where this would all end. Or if it ever would.

• • •

I had been too distracted to shop for gifts and once back home I realized that I had to make an emergency run to the mall that afternoon, Christmas Eve. Linda decided that we should all go so the kids could see Santa, which they had done annually until the previous year. While Anthony had decided the last Christmas before he got sick that Santa was fictitious, eight-year-old Alex still believed in him and had a list to deliver. Don readied Anthony for the outing and transferred him into the front seat of my SUV while I stored his wheelchair in the back. The five of us rode the few miles to Kenwood Towne Center.

At about two o'clock, the mall was busy with last-minute shoppers like me. I parked the SUV in a handicapped slot close to the entrance on the lower level of the mall and retrieved Anthony's wheelchair while Don transferred him out of the front seat. Anthony desperately needed a haircut and he was bound for the hair salon just inside the mall doors while I went about my shopping.

I found gifts for each of them. Alex was easy to buy for, loving the most feminine apparel and glittery objects, and The Limited Too supplied the most current fashions in jeans and tops. Easy to please, at her young age, she made everyone feel good about the gifts they had given by announcing enthusiastically, "This is perfect. It's exactly what I wanted!"

Linda was just the opposite of Alex. She was quite

pragmatic and not into "bling" so I bought her what I buy every year, the softest of flannel pajamas from Victoria Secret.

Buying for Anthony was tough. He couldn't use his hands and didn't have an affinity for much of anything these days. He had a huge collection of t-shirts because this was an obviously useful gift for any teenage boy and he was accumulating a selection of videos he seemed to enjoy now that his eyes were better able to focus.

As I wandered the mall, I passed the Gamestop store, where he and I had hung out in our prior life, perusing the shelves and making plans for our next game purchase. He clearly wasn't ready for video games, but I still held out hope that we would play together again someday. Eventually, I bought a silver crucifix that he could wear around his neck and a Michael Jordan poster. Less than perfect, but I couldn't think of anything else.

I made my way back toward the food court, our designated meeting place. As I approached, Linda saw me. She, Don, Anthony and Alex headed in the direction of Santa where we all got into a line. There were several other parties ahead of us, but it moved quickly. I imagined that Santa was ready for his gig to be up by four o'clock on Christmas Eve and he was wasting no time moving his young visitors through.

Linda wanted a photo of the kids with Santa for our collection of the past thirteen years, so Don pushed Anthony up the ramp to sit beside Santa while Alex climbed into his lap. Don had just placed Anthony where his wheelchair would fit, a little to the right and front of Santa when a funny thing happened. Anthony got very excited. Looking at Santa, his face lit up, he broke into a huge smile and lifted his arms above his head.

Anthony had suddenly recognized Santa! In a flash, he had

remembered this prominent childhood figure. He knew that Santa represented good things, happy times, gifts, tradition. Somewhere deep inside of him memories had been buried. Being there and seeing Santa had triggered those memories.

In that moment maybe he recalled every Christmas since he was three, or maybe Santa only helped him remember his past excitement as each gift-giving day approached. We would never know because he would never be able to tell us. But as I looked at the Polaroid photograph inside the tacky red and green cardboard frame, the sheer excitement and naked joy in Anthony's face gave evidence that he had journeyed a long way in a single moment.

CHAPTER 27

"Yeah Baby!"

JANUARY 2000

Super Bowl Sunday, January, 30, 2000, Rams vs. Titans. We were watching the game in our family room, which ran along the southern end of the house, front to back. It was a comfortable cheerful room, with white plantation shuttered windows, yellow walls, white trim and a tweed-colored carpet. The back window looked out over the deep wooded yard. The front window provided views of a quiet, tree-lined street with mature, well-kept homes and lawns that led to the cul-de-sac.

With four bedrooms, two full and two half bathrooms and a large basement it was spacious for the four of us and when we bought it, we thought we would be there for a long time. However, we had to rethink our plans; Anthony needed more privacy than the family room provided him, and we needed this community space.

The area still served as our family room. We had simply rearranged the gray awning-striped sofa, loveseat and tan leather recliner to accommodate Anthony's medical bed and equipment. Located to the right of a small foyer as one came in the front door, this room was a hub of activity.

We had wanted Anthony to be in the midst of everything and he was. Family, friends, neighbors, nurses and therapists were in and out of our house and his makeshift room, day and night. Since he had never wanted to miss any "goings-on" and had nearly always been part of any gathering or conversation, this was as close as we could get to honoring his previous lifestyle.

My brother Ray was in town to watch the Super Bowl with us, as he was nearly every year. Anthony was laying on his back on a mat on the carpeted floor in front of us, taking a much needed "butt break", after sitting in his wheelchair for a couple hours. The three of us were watching the game together. At least Ray and I were watching the football game. We weren't always sure if Anthony was able to focus well enough to see what was on the screen. The neurologist told us that his eyes had probably been affected by the lack of oxygen, but at this point it was impossible to get reliable and consistent responses from Anthony that would enable the ophthalmologist to diagnose his vision.

It was halftime, which meant chili time. Chili time in our world happens on three special occasions every year. The first is New Year's Day. The second accompanies the Super Bowl and the third occasion is in March and includes the opening and qualifying round of the NCAA Tournament, "March Madness." Each time I get ready for these big events by purchasing huge quantities of flank steak, ground pork and Italian sausage. A chili connoisseur, I had discovered an exceptional recipe when Linda and I volunteered several years ago for A Gourmet Sensation, an annual fundraiser held each year by Hospice of Cincinnati. The event brings in well known chefs from famous restaurants located around the country to reproduce some of

their best loved recipes. Hospice publishes these recipes in an annual cookbook, which we bought whenever we volunteered.

I had expanded Kevin Garvin's original "Flank Steak Chili with Black Beans" recipe into my own well-respected version, otherwise known as "Tony's Three-Alarm Trifecta" because it included three different meats along with several types of peppers. A task I always enjoyed, this thrice yearly undertaking included the chopping and sautéing of vegetables and grilling of different meats until our house was infused with a delicious aroma that made your mouth water. It also required that you regularly sample large quantities from the different pots to ensure that each "Trifecta" was, indeed, underway. Ideally, I started cooking the day before the big event so that the ingredients in each of the three different pots—one of which included the original, unadulterated Trifecta version, another a turkey or vegetarian version, and a third one, which included a less spicy version—had adequate time to meld together. The result was a hot, but blissful assault on the taste buds that, when accompanied by ice cold beer, produced a thoroughly enjoyable, sweat producing and memorable experience.

After getting Anthony off the floor and into his wheelchair, Ray and I went to the kitchen for chili. Still unable to eat much of anything beyond bland, well pureed mashed potatoes or ice cream, Anthony's food intake consisted mostly of liquid nutritional supplement that he took through his g-tube during the many hours that he spent in bed. He didn't seem to know or care that he was missing out on chili.

Ray and I each came back into the room with a tray, which held a bowl of original recipe Trifecta topped with shredded cheese and Frito corn chips, alongside a hotdog, and a bottle of Coors beer. As Ray sat down, he caught a glimpse of the Rams

cheerleaders doing their halftime presentation and said, "Anthony, what do you think of that?"

Incredibly, Anthony replied, "Yeah baby."

"What did you say?" I asked Anthony and while I waited for him to respond, I yelled to Linda.

"Ray, did he just talk?" I asked my brother.

Ray and I looked at each other, eyes wide. Anthony had just spoken for the first time since September 8, 1998, nearly sixteen months ago.

As Linda, Jeni and Grandma came running into the room, Ray and I tried to tell them that Anthony had spoken, but we were both talking simultaneously.

"You're not going to believe this. Anthony just said 'Yeah baby.'"

"Really?" Linda asked, as she looked back and forth from me to Ray to Anthony, unconvinced.

"He did! Didn't he, Ray?" I said.

Ray nodded. "I saw the cheerleaders on TV and asked Anthony what he thought of that. And he said 'Yeah baby.'"

"Anthony, can you say it again?" Linda asked. Anthony sat there looking back at her.

"I think you two are hallucinating." Linda said.

They dismissed us since he didn't speak again, figuring we were imagining things, that the Super Bowl and the beer had contributed to our wishful thinking. But Ray and I knew we had heard him speak.

On Monday Mrs. Dinardo called to excitedly tell us that Anthony surprised everyone when she had asked the class the sum of five plus five, and, to everyone's surprise, he had responded with, "Ten."

Shortly after that he began to reciprocate our "hellos", and

he started to answer "yes" and "no" questions. He delighted Linda's sister, when one night a few weeks after the Super Bowl, she came into his room and he said, "Hi, Aunt Jeni." For months, Jeni had been telling him that the first time he initiated and greeted her, she would pay him $100. She happily paid the bribe.

Linda had mentioned that she was working with the doctors to take Anthony off of some of his medications because Bev, his most holistic nurse, felt that he might be over medicated. I wondered how much these recent med changes had contributed to Anthony's sudden ability to speak.

We had been in the process of getting insurance approval for a Dynavox, a visual communication board that displays the letters of the alphabet. Anthony's speech therapist, Sandra Grether, had been working several times a week teaching him to use a laser pointer positioned on his forehead to spell out words a letter at a time. This was an absurd task because Anthony had no real head and neck control and consequently the laser light moved erratically and unpredictably. But because it had been more than sixteen months since he had spoken a single word, this had seemed the only solution that might allow him to communicate at all.

Anthony's "Yeah baby" was significant for many reasons, the first, most obvious one being that he had actually been able to speak, a complex action that requires thought and coordination of brain, tongue, lips and mouth. However, the fact that he was aware of the cheerleaders prancing across a nineteen-inch television screen was also noteworthy. We knew that his vision had been affected by the lack of oxygen to his brain, but we had had no way of knowing exactly how well he was able to see.

Lastly, we were encouraged that he said, "Yeah baby,"

recalling the catch phrase that is used throughout the Austin Powers movie "The Spy Who Shagged Me" and reiterated throughout the day by Don. It told us that Anthony was retaining certain things and that he did have a semblance of a memory.

His ability to speak a few words represented a major event in Anthony's recovery, one that evidenced progress in an otherwise depressingly unconstructive sixteen months. Needless to say, we were overjoyed by his utterance for so many reasons. Most importantly, we wanted him to be able to talk. Language being the foundation upon which all else rests, we felt that as long as he could talk, he could tell us what he needed; if he was uncomfortable, hungry or thirsty. To be sealed off from the world, unable to communicate in any human engagement, was a torturous, unfathomable fate. The fact that Anthony had developed the ability to coordinate his tongue, his lips and his thoughts well enough to utter even a few words, gave us renewed hope that he would recover.

Little by little, Anthony regained some speech, and although his diction was less than perfect, this recently recovered ability renewed our dedication and commitment to his rehabilitation. We were relieved that he was beginning to interact verbally and happily cancelled the order for the Dynavox. We concentrated our efforts on strengthening his tongue and perfecting the use of his lips and breathing patterns so that he would develop his ability to converse.

We began to include Anthony in conversations, waiting patiently for his delayed response to the "yes" and "no" questions we posed for him, and after dinner we would practice singing jingles he knew, like that of the Kit Kat candy bar. I would start: "Give me a break." Linda would follow: "Give me a break." Alex

would sing: "Break me off a piece of that ..." Anthony would finish with "Kit Kat Bar."

One of our favorite ads had been the famous Super Bowl Budweiser commercial that included Freddie and Louis, the swamp frog and lizard who had conversations that emulated those of a couple of guys in a bar. Anthony and I used to play the parts of the different characters before he had gotten sick and so he knew each of the routines. Now, Alex and I each played the parts of Frankie and Louis and at the end the two of us would belch out the following syllables in succession— "Bud," then "weis." We left it to Anthony to fill in the "er."

Communication became our number one goal.

CHAPTER 28

Mom and Dad in the Hospital

FEBRUARY 2000

It was February 11 and I was headed to Manchester once again. According to the Weather Channel, I would be exchanging one bitter, grey wintery day in Cincinnati for another. However, I was looking forward to this trip because Tim had arranged a dinner for the six producers who had qualified for the Pinnacle Club, affording us the opportunity to celebrate privately before the main event in May. I looked forward to an evening of camaraderie. I would leave my coach-teacher hat at the office while we ate, drank and congratulated each other on last year's accomplishments.

The flight was uneventful and I arrived mid-morning, in time to conduct the afternoon group training session. At five o'clock we finished and headed for the parking lot. Tim and I got into his black Audi TT roadster, the latest of his car purchases. In the time I had known Tim, he had owned three different vehicles, each one sportier than the last, and I envied his latest purchase, even while my six-foot-four-inch frame wasn't exactly built to fit its low to the ground, compact interior.

Tim drove to our favorite dinner spot, CR Sparks Restaurant. We parked and entered the restaurant in time to meet four of the six qualifying producers: Mickey, Tom, Dick and Sandy. The restaurant was expecting us. Drinks were ordered and as they arrived, the other two producers, Chris and Jerry, joined us at the table. More drinks and appetizers were ordered.

As I sat to the right of Tim, at the head of the long rectangular table, I felt a sense of satisfaction. The producers were clearly excited that they had qualified for Pinnacle Club and were anticipating a warm get-away with their spouses in Boca Raton. In the process of qualifying, each had benefitted financially, increasing their income, as they had worked to reach that goal.

It felt good to know that I had contributed to their success, and ultimately, to their happiness. I knew first-hand how difficult the rejection of prospecting was; getting up each morning, knowing that I had to make twenty or thirty calls that day, hoping to find a spark of interest during one of them. I knew, too well, the emotional roller coaster ride that a potential buyer could cause; their waffling on a decision, or even worse, they're using me for information while buying from a competitor. I identified with these people. I had walked in their shoes.

I also knew how great it felt to make a sale, to find just the right solution for a client's specific situation. I knew how it felt to be regarded as a valued expert. I knew the highs and the lows these salespeople experienced daily.

I also loved the chase. I loved closing the deal. But mostly I loved the control over my income and my lifestyle that selling gave me. I knew that some of these producers, like Dick, had realized the same thing a long time ago, while others were just recognizing that their lifestyles were dependent upon their disciplined prospecting and selling activities.

Linda's confronting me about my lack of prospecting activity had ended my hiatus. I was back to making daily calls and meeting with potential clients. I felt good about my activity once again, even if we weren't seeing results yet. Before Anthony's illness, we had grown accustomed to an income that afforded us what we wanted. I remembered a few years ago, telling Linda to go ahead and buy her mom and dad's house if she wanted; the money would show up. I would make it show up, and I did. Shortly after we bought it, our income had doubled. I had sold more business than we needed for the mortgage and additional expenses of a bigger home.

My reflections were interrupted by Mickey's gregarious toast: "Here's to Boca and Pinnacle Club. May this be the first of many to come." We all raised our glasses. Conversation followed, mostly shop talk. But as the drinks took effect, business gave way to good-natured ribbing and soon, we were all laughing heartily at the stories that were told.

A couple of hours later, Tim drove me back to the Holiday Inn. In route, I told him about my speaking at Pinnacle Club, but since Sandra and I had decided to keep Anthony's presence a secret until we brought him on stage, I asked him to keep this to himself. We made plans to play golf and have dinner together while we were in Boca Raton. I said goodnight as I got out of the car. I would see him in the morning when I came to the office for my scheduled one-on-one meetings with the producers.

Back in the hotel room, I checked the messages on my cell phone. My sister, Tresa, had called, asking me to call her. She often called to say "hello" and since it was nearly eleven o'clock, I decided to call her in the morning.

When I reached Tresa on Friday morning during a break

between meetings, she told me that Mom and Dad were both in the hospital. They had been diagnosed with pneumonia. Since they had been robust cigarette smokers from a young age, and often had upper respiratory illnesses, I wasn't surprised. Usually they recovered, but this time, they must have gotten a bug that had lodged in their lungs, possibly aggravated by the incessant cigarette smoke circulating in their little house during the harsh New York winter. This time they had both had trouble breathing when my brother Michael decided to take them to the hospital.

Tresa wasn't too concerned, but was heading there from her home in Hammonton, New Jersey for the weekend. She said she'd keep me posted on their status. I went back to my meetings. My parents were in their mid-sixties and I wondered how much longer they would be around. At noon, I called Linda and told her about Mom and Dad. I suggested that since I was in the Northeast, maybe I should go and visit over the weekend. She agreed. I called Delta and arranged to fly into Syracuse. I would have to rent a car and drive the hour and a half to Norwich but I had done this several times before and was comfortable with the drive, even late at night.

I got to Norwich close to midnight. I had talked to Tresa while driving and she told me she had visited our parents shortly before visiting hours were over. Mom and Dad were on IV fluids and were resting well. They were in good spirits when she and my nephew, Kevin, left the hospital at nine p.m. I checked into the Howard Johnson motel just a couple miles away, called Linda to let her know I had gotten there safely, climbed into bed and fell fast asleep.

On Saturday morning I woke up, grabbed some coffee and headed to Chenango Memorial Hospital, a small regional

hospital which I had visited previously for stitches when I had slit my finger open while filleting a fish.

I found Mom and Dad's room easily in the small two-story hospital. They were both awake, no doubt wondering where the coffee was and when they could smoke again, since that was their early morning habit. I popped my head into the room.

"Hello, Mom and Dad," I said.

"Anthony, what are you doing here?" Mom asked.

My family had always called me Anthony, which actually came out sounding more like "Antny." I had taken the nickname "Tony" in college and had used it since.

"Son-of-a-bitch and I'll be damned. Look who's here," Dad swore, like he had done in practically every sentence I had ever heard him utter.

"Tresa called yesterday and said you both were in the hospital. Since I was already in New Hampshire, I thought I'd stop by and see you," I said.

My dad got out of bed and came around to hug me, dragging his IV pole with him. I bent down to embrace him since he was quite a bit shorter than I. How he and my mom had produced me, at six-foot-four, and Ray, who was six-foot-seven, was a genetic mystery. We had heard that Mom, who was adopted, had had tall birth relatives whom we had never met.

"Antny, we had a time of it. Damned good thing Michael got us here when he did. Son-of-a-bitch were we sick!" Dad said, hoarsely.

"Is he driving the nurses crazy yet?" I asked my mom, as I bent down to kiss her cheek. She smiled and shook her head.

"You know your dad. He can't sit still," she replied.

"How is 'Little Squanto'? How are you?" she asked. Little Squanto was the American Indian name my parents had given Anthony.

Years before, Mom and Dad had adopted Native American culture. They now spent hours crafting Indian dolls and bead-work, listening to audio cassette tapes of American Indian folklore and lilting flute melodies. They had befriended a tribesman, who was known as Chief Running Horse, and regularly visited a nearby reservation. The last time we'd been to see them, they had renewed their wedding vows in a traditional Native American ceremony, complete with Chief Running Horse and peace pipe. The rituals, music and words chanted were foreign and fascinating to us, but were of particular interest to the kids, who thought the Chief was very cool.

"I'm fine. Anthony is doing better. He has started to talk a little bit, mostly responding to questions," I said. I didn't want to tell the whole story. There was no reason for it. My parents hadn't seen Anthony since before he had gotten sick. They probably wouldn't see him unless I found a way to get him up here because they never travelled outside of New York, New Jersey and Pennsylvania. I didn't know when or if they would ever see each other again.

Tresa and Kevin entered the room and my sister's boisterous voice interrupted our conversation.

"How was your night?" Tresa embraced Dad, who was still standing beside me next to Mom's bed.

"Jesus Christ, I don't know how anybody gets any better here. You can't sleep. God-damn, son-of-a-bitch nurses in and out all night long!" Dad groused good-naturedly. While he had always been a character, in recent years, my dad had become downright "colorful" and was now often mistaken for Willy

Nelson, with his tattoos and hair braids, beaded headbands and bear claw necklaces.

Tresa turned to me. "Hi, big brother. Glad you were able to get here," she said, as we hugged. We were eleven months apart and she liked to remind me regularly that I was the elder.

"Kevin, what's up?" I turned to greet my thirteen-year-old, dark-haired nephew, who had hugged Grandpa and was standing beside him. Kevin was just a couple months younger than Anthony and we had always coordinated our New York visits with Tresa's family because Anthony, Kevin and Kevin's brother, Brian, were all close in age and were inseparable from the time they got together until the time we left.

When I looked at Kevin, it all came back to me. Anthony's blank stare, his bed ridden state, his incontinence. This was the way it always happened. I would unknowingly forget for a while. Then without warning, it was like a truck smashed violently into my consciousness and I would experience the shock, the reality of the emptiness, of the Anthony I had loved, of the Anthony I hadn't seen in over a year.

It's not Kevin's fault, I told myself. I hid the cacophony of emotion taking place inside my head, the deafening noise in my ears, as I saw the past summers of Anthony, Kevin and Brian hanging out together, playing homerun derby in the side yard of my parents' little red house, fishing at the creek. It all flashed through my mind as my throat tightened and I struggled to breathe.

At this point, my brother Ray was the only one in my family who had visited and so he was the only one who knew firsthand Anthony's devastating condition. The rest of the family really didn't have a clue, didn't know, and probably didn't want to know just how bad things were. I didn't blame them.

The essence of a beloved child gone, now an empty shell was too difficult to assimilate.

If I don't look, I won't know and then it can't happen to my child. I understood this irrational strategy within any sane parent's mind. I would do the same in their shoes. I would go on with my life, pretending that this incredible life changing, mind altering event hadn't happened to someone I loved. I would put it out of my head although I might pay it lip service by saying aloud, "Boy, are we blessed." But never, for a moment, would I know just how truly blessed I was.

I spent several hours each of the next three days at the hospital. Mom assured me that she and Dad would be fine as she patted my hand. She told me I should go home. I should take care of my family. She looked tired. She was starting to show her age, but she was in good spirits.

The rest of the time I spent at their little red house, where Tresa and Kevin were staying. We visited late into the night, talking and listening to music. The small place seemed empty without my dad's larger-than-life character and my mom's quiet, gentle nurturing. But I introduced Kevin, who was a gifted musician, to the greatness of Johnny Cash and the "Folsom Prison Blues" and I'm sure he will forever be thankful.

• • •

A couple of weeks later, back in Cincinnati, I was in the kitchen drying and putting away dishes. I called my parents to see how they were doing. They were fine, watching Thursday night college football, thankful to be home and in their own bed. We talked about my coming out in the spring as I always did. I hung up relieved that they were well, glad that I had called.

Mom died the following morning. Heart attack. She had said she wasn't feeling too well and had gone to take a shower, thinking it would make her feel better. Dad found her a little while later on the floor of their bedroom.

I was shocked. I had just talked to her and she sounded fine. I immediately wondered how long my dad would last without her. They had been inseparable since us kids had been out of the house. I imagined him walking from room to room, searching for signs of her, remembering her each time he found one.

In the last year I had learned that tragedies were never expected and I was never going to be prepared for one. Still, I was reeling from the disappearance of Anthony and I couldn't let myself mourn the death of my mother. I was afraid that if I gave into the sadness that I would be swept up in a sea of despair from which I might never recover.

I travelled to Norwich once again. My mother had been cremated, as had been her wish. My sister-in-law, Elizabeth, had painted a beautiful eagle on a ceramic urn that now contained her ashes. Chief Running Horse led the Native American funeral ceremony on a rare, sunny, but frigid afternoon in upstate New York. Afterward, Mom's urn sat at the table with us while my brothers, sister, dad and I visited, drank, remembered and cried. We all got sufficiently drunk and decided that her remains should be placed in the pantry. Corn, tomatoes, beans, Mom. She would have laughed right along with us.

In the end, Dad built a shrine on the table for her, his lovely mourning dove, his partner of fifty-one years. She sat where we would all be reminded of her gentle ways.

CHAPTER 29

Anthony Cries

MARCH 2000

I started working on a blueberry farm where my dad was fore-man when I was five years old. Ray Cole Sr. was demanding, disciplined and hard working. He expected me to live up to his strict standards, even as a kid. He taught my brothers, my sis-ter and I that hard work produced results. He accepted no ex-cuses from us or from anyone else. Farm life didn't allow for excuses.

I worked long hours just like the rest of the farmhands. At five a.m., I was up and working the fields with my siblings and two to three hundred migrant workers. I took pride in my abil-ity to work alongside the much older men and women who picked and packed the blueberries. By age ten, I could outwork them all and I followed my dad whenever possible, watching him, learning everything I could. By the age of thirteen, I was driving tractors and giving directions to the workers.

Like my dad, I accepted no excuses from my clients or from my family and despite his changed condition, I accepted no ex-cuses from Anthony. I continued to work my son hard when I

was home on weekends, knowing that eventually he would respond and improve his physical and mental abilities. I continued to be in his face regularly when I was in town, challenging him.

One Sunday afternoon Bev, the nurse on duty, and I were working with Anthony in his gait trainer, a large walker on wheels that provided adjustable support through a seat, armrests and various attachments. I had stretched his legs in preparation for our session. I talked to him, coached him, readying him for today's therapy. I stood him up and Bev pushed the walker into place. Together, we strapped Anthony's forearms to the supports, and tethered his ankles to the guides that kept his steps aligned.

As Anthony leaned into the armrests, his agitation already obvious, I prompted him to initiate steps, a seemingly simple process which he could do on rare occasions, but never consistently. Today he followed my command and hesitantly lifted his right foot while bearing weight on his left. Bev guided his suspended foot a few inches forward and placed it on the floor.

Taking a step with his left leg was always the bigger challenge. Since the time of his heart attack, Anthony had developed what is known as extensor tone in his left leg and we had come to rely on this leg to support his weight while he stood and transferred to and from bed. Unfortunately, his right leg contracted at the knee, and he knew enough not to trust it to support him. Lifting his left leg to take a step was scary because this was the one that he knew he could depend upon to keep him from falling.

To make matters worse, Anthony's sense of balance and his spatial orientation had changed. He no longer made the connection that his feet were on the same floor that spread out in front of him. We didn't know whether he actually felt the

ground through the soles of his feet, and the floor ahead of him might well have been broken into pieces, since the ophthalmologist suspected "field cuts" in Anthony's vision. Despite all of this, I was sure that, with enough practice, he would come to trust that the ground wouldn't move and would remember his ability to walk.

This was turning out to be a particularly unsuccessful session and after using every coaching technique I knew, I found myself yelling at Anthony, telling him that he wasn't trying hard enough, that he needed to work harder, that he would never improve if he didn't give every thing he had. Finally, frustrated to the core, I called him a "slacker." I told him that he could stay in his wheelchair forever if that was what he wanted. I stomped away leaving Bev, stricken but accustomed to my outbursts, to get Anthony into his chair.

I was still angry a couple of hours later when Bev brought Anthony to the kitchen before she left for the evening. I continued to berate him for his lack of effort. Anthony sat there staring back at me as I lectured.

But a few minutes later, he started to sob. Sobs that took his breath away. Woeful howls from his soul. As I put together a word here and there, I realized he was asking me 'why I hated him.' Frustrated because he couldn't translate his feelings into words, he had become distraught, sobbing louder and louder until he was wailing. Tears streamed down his face. He was totally inconsolable. I tried to explain that I was working him hard to make him better. But he just wouldn't listen. He wouldn't calm down.

"Leave him alone. Stop talking." Linda commanded, as she stood next to Anthony. She had been setting the table when Anthony had started to cry.

"He's fine," I said.

"You're making it worse," she glared

Anthony was crying so hard he had begun to hiccup. His shirt, wet with tears, his arms drawn up tight and his face contorted, he was beyond my control. Finally, Linda took him into our bedroom and closed the door, separating him from me, making me stay in the kitchen until she could soothe Anthony. It was probably fifteen minutes later that she opened the bedroom door.

Later we sat down to eat dinner, but with little appetite. Our Sunday meals usually included Grandma and Jeni, but they had left for home. Too painful to watch Anthony suffer, they were helpless to interfere in our private family crisis. They left, affording us our privacy.

While Anthony accepted my explanation and apology, his nearly nonexistent short-term memory helping him to forget his earlier emotional upheaval, it was several hours before Linda would speak to me or look me in the eye. I could tell she hadn't left the incident behind as she entered the master bedroom after readying Anthony for the night.

"Tony, you were totally out of line today. Every time you work with Anthony, it's the same thing. He's trying his hardest, but he just can't do what you want him to do. You are torturing him and all of us," she said, as she stood with her arms crossed, glaring at me.

"You don't know what you're talking about. Nobody is working him hard enough. That's the problem. You have spoiled him. Now he's lazy. He responds for me because I push him hard like I always have. That's the only way he will get better," I retorted.

"You think you're making him better? You're not making

him better. You scare him to death. He gets so upset when you're around that he can't do anything at all." She countered.

"Fine. Then he's never going to get out of that wheelchair. He needs to work harder and longer. He needs to want it more," I was getting angrier.

"You are ruining your relationship with him. He is glad when you're out of town and you're not here making him feel like dirt. We all are. Life is easier when you're gone," she said.

"You're right. Life *is* easier when I'm gone!" I agreed emphatically.

"Alex came to me crying tonight, asking 'Why is Daddy so mean to Anthony?' She asked me to make you stop. This isn't the first time. You're making everybody miserable. I won't stand by and let you take your frustration out on the kids. You had better figure it out soon," she demanded, as she turned away and walked toward the bathroom.

"Or what? You'll divorce me?" I followed her. "Like you have any options." I was tired of her telling me what to do.

"Yes." She turned around to face me and said calmly. "If I have to. And we will be fine. Without you."

I was irate. Already angry at the lack of control I had over my life and family, I picked up my battery-operated toothbrush and in a fit of rage, threw it. It narrowly missed her head and carved a chunk out of the wall behind her.

CHAPTER 30

Tony on the Ice Cube

The brain is an amazing organ. As the control center to all parts south, with the slightest desire, it enables one to pick up a foot, take a step, and keep the body upright while simultaneously moving arms in opposite directions, still supplying the necessary physics to keep one's balance. While regulating body temperature, kidney function, blinking the eyes and allowing one to hold a conversation on a cell phone that is held in one's hand, the brain decodes sounds that come through the earpiece and within nanoseconds forms a thought and a verbal response. Most of us take all of this for granted, being able to control the private universe of our own mind and body.

The brain also allows us the capacity to feel, to imagine, to pretend. It has the ability to transport us to another world through movies or books. It allows us to become someone else for a short time, giving us a reprieve from our own lives, and it inspires and educates us to evolve into different people with its ability to absorb and recall, enhancing our jobs, our families, our lives.

When a person sustains a brain injury, all of these functions may be affected. In the case of Anthony, who suffers from anoxic brain injury, or lack of oxygen, the damage is global which means that virtually everything—bodily functions, intelligence, physical ability, sight, memory, etc. is damaged. Anthony's injury, like each and every brain injury, is unique. A person's ability to recover and function after an assault depends largely upon the extent and location of the damage.

Anthony's heart attack nearly killed him. But the real problem, lack of oxygen, catapulted him into a coma that lasted many months and, in the end, left him a different person. We were blessed in that Anthony's basic personality had remained intact. This is not always the case. Often personalities change drastically. Anthony is, and was, typically friendly and warm. In other words, he will look at you and initiate a conversation, although it may not always be relevant to that particular moment or to anything you might be interested in knowing. But he strives to connect with you in his unique way.

Imagine that Anthony is frozen in a big ice cube, an ice cube that he looks out of, that lends a blurry quality to what he sees, what he thinks. He is unable to make his arms and legs, even his tongue, obey basic commands. Early on, this ice cube prevents him from having control over anything at all.

I see him too, frozen in this ice cube, staring back at me, at first not even recognizing who I am. I try to break through the ice, jump up and down in front of it, in front of him. When that doesn't work, I jump on the ice, hit it with my fists, kick it and otherwise continue to pound away at this façade that separates him, my boy, from me.

When I realize I can't get through the ice, I try yelling, hoping he can hear me through this thick, unrelenting barrier. Over

time, it becomes clear that I am not getting through, I'm not going to get through, and I see my angry, aggravated face in the blurry reflection of the ice cube, this obstacle that prevents me from reaching Anthony.

In the meantime, I spend hours and days building regimens that, in my experience as an athletic coach, will contribute to his ability to stand or to walk. I coach Anthony as I had coached athletes in the past, pushing and cajoling and berating him to overcome his weaknesses, to work harder, all the while thinking that he isn't working to his true ability, that he is holding out on me.

By this time, Anthony has moments of real clarity. In one of those moments, he cries because he is distraught that he cannot please me, cannot do what I demand of him. In the days following that terrible night, I realize that I have become relentless and unreasonable in my demands of him. I finally understand the extent of his injury. At last I recognize that he is absolutely incapable of doing what I wish for him to do.

CHAPTER 31

Back at Pinnacle Club

MAY 13, 2000

Last December it seemed like a great idea to present an inspirational message with Anthony at the USI top producer conference. But as I stood backstage waiting for my cue to go on, I was less certain. It has been well over a year and a half since Anthony had his heart attack, since he had fallen into a coma.

Only recently had he gained a limited ability to speak. His diction is hard to understand, his mental processing slow. He has no aptitude for remembering a script. In the short time since he started speaking again, I have learned that his answers to questions are not always what one might expect. So, while I am rehearsed in my part of the presentation, his responses will be entirely spontaneous. I am nervous because I'm just not sure what he will say.

Since Anthony is still disoriented in time and place, he doesn't remember that it is Saturday, that we are in Boca Raton, Florida, and that we will be speaking to nearly one hundred and thirty people. But he is aware enough to be excited about working with me. He is excited because for years he has

dreamed of the time when he would represent Anthony Cole Training alongside his dad. That day has finally come, although I don't think either of us would have envisioned it this way.

"Please welcome my son and our special guest today, Anthony Cole, Jr."

At this point, Don, the nurse, pushes Anthony onto the stage. Nearly all of the audience has heard of Anthony's disability, but most have never met him and do not know he is present. They reward him with a standing ovation that goes on for several minutes. Many are openly crying and it takes all my powers of concentration to control my emotions as I see Anthony's thrilled expression.

After the applause dies down, I am able to engage him in conversation and ask him a few questions. "Anthony, not long ago you returned to junior high. Can you tell us what you like about school?"

"Girls," he says.

Even though he is wired with a microphone, Anthony's new speech is hard to understand, so I must translate most of what he says. I am looking for another answer and I ask again, "Aside from girls, what do you like about school?"

"Just girls," he says.

Not unusual for a thirteen-year-old boy. At this point, I'm thinking 'this isn't going where I thought it would.' I decide I'm going to try one more time. So I ask him, "Anthony, let's suppose we were on the moon and you were going to school where there were no girls. What would you like best?" I'm praying that he comes through. And he does.

"Then why would I go to the moon?" His answer brings the house down.

We turn to more serious topics. I remind Anthony that he

has had to relearn everything—from blowing his nose to talking. When I ask him what he likes about physical therapy he replies bluntly, "Nothing. It is hard." But he acknowledges that these therapies are helping him improve bit by bit, making him stronger, teaching him how to eat and talk again, pushing him to do what he otherwise would be incapable of doing.

In Anthony's world there are no magic leaps of progress. His own *kaizen*, his own personal journey of incremental and never ending improvement, requires him to labor at every aspect of his limited physical and mental abilities. He has to work to manage his trunk and balance to sit upright in his wheelchair. He struggles to absorb, process, compose and deliver "yes" and "no" answers to questions. The simple act of scratching an itchy eye requires major effort to coordinate spastic muscles to facilitate relief, which he is sometimes unable to do.

His brain was so affected on September 8 that nothing is easily learned or implemented. Anthony can't remember what happened as little as three hours ago, so he can't compare yesterday's therapy session to today's. He no longer has the ability to plan for tomorrow, so he can't think ahead to dream that the next day or the next year things will be better. All he has is today, right now. Yet if you were to ask him how he is, he would inevitably smile, say "Great" and work to engage you in conversation, hoping to draw you in, to make a most valuable human-to-human connection.

While he doesn't have a memory, he does know that once upon a time he nearly died. He has never forgotten this. He knows that what matters are the people around him. Accepting of everyone, his unconditional love for all comes from a place that few of us have ever seen. A place at the door of death.

Perhaps this is Anthony's lesson for us all—to live in this

particular moment in time, to focus on loving and connecting with those important before they are taken from us. Or we, from them.

I tell the audience that we have small posters for them. On the poster is an outline of Anthony's hand and the title of today's presentation *Ignite the Fire Within*. I invite the participants to take one and tape it to the doorframe of their offices. I hope that each time they leave, they will put their hand to Anthony's and be reminded to make that precious human-to-human connection, as they go about their day.

In the meantime, Don stands behind Anthony as he sits in his wheelchair at the exit to deliver "high-fives" in person. Anthony is limited in his ability to use his arms so his "high-fives" are aided by Don. Nearly everyone comes by to greet him, to shake his contracted hand, to thank him for being here.

Others come to the podium to thank me for a unique inspirational message. A salesperson from New York City approaches tearfully, saying she wants to retire and raise her young daughter. Another participant tells me that his wife is flying home immediately to be with the kids as a result of the presentation. "Thanks a lot," he says, sarcastically. But his empathetic smile tells me he is okay with it.

A slide presentation of Anthony's long journey since September 8, set to the music "I Believe I Can Fly" from his favorite movie, "Space Jam" plays on the screen. I walk to the back of the room, watching him charm the people who gather around.

As I get closer, his eyes meet mine. As tears slide down my cheeks, I nod my head and smile, telling him wordlessly, how proud I am of him. How proud I am to be his father.

CHAPTER 32

Slow-to-Learn Lessons

JANUARY 2010

Looking back, I see that as I searched for the boy I held next to my heart, I lost sight of everything else. My internal compass kept pointing me to the child who left for school on September 8, 1998. My drive to regain that firstborn son nearly cost me my family and my business.

I didn't want to believe that Anthony had changed, that he was anything less than the perfect, shining son he had entered the world as. I refused to believe the doctors who told me that his devastating event would permanently disable him. When the Children's chief neurologist told me that Anthony would have a twenty percent chance of living independently, I demanded a new neurologist, one who would believe, along with me, that Anthony would recover fully. It was simply inconceivable that the outcome would be anything less.

I had worked with Anthony, taught him, coached him all his young life. I knew his potential. I knew he worked hard to perfect his skills so that he would receive a nod or a positive comment from me. He lived for my approval. I had high

standards and living up to these standards was a difficult task for anyone, let alone a kid with a debilitating brain injury. Yet I chose to ignore the reality of his limitations, forcing him to accomplish the impossible goals I had set for him, demeaning him when he couldn't.

In the days that followed Anthony's breakdown and my own violent behavior, I fell deeply into despair. As I searched my soul, I came to understand what Anthony already knew; that my love for him was conditional, that my love and approval were based upon what he could do, what he could be, that would make me proud. Since he wasn't able to perform well enough to please me, he knew he had lost my endorsement. His father's love and approval had been replaced by an endless string of miserable conflicts. My love had been withdrawn.

It became clear that my efforts to rehabilitate him weren't entirely directed at improving his function and ability. Much of my real motivation came from the desire to make him the perfectly formed person he was when he left to catch the bus on that fateful September morning. As if making him walk could restore him.

It took me a long time to see my own reflection in the ice, to recognize that my behavior was unproductive and destructive. I could not let go my idea of that radiant son, the handsome, bright and emerging adult that Anthony was becoming prior to his heart attack. My resolute determination to regain this person I had loved so intensely kept me from seeing that he had changed forever. I am ashamed that during this lengthy process, I tortured him and those I loved and cared for in my selfish quest to resurrect Anthony.

My first son had effectively died on the playground. That Anthony was never coming back. The best doctors in the world

couldn't bring him back. I couldn't bring him back. That Anthony was gone forever.

It was in the terrible dark days after Anthony's breakdown, that I began to find my courage. The courage to stop pounding away at the ice. The courage to stop berating Anthony for his lack of ability. It was during those hellish moments that I was jolted into the realization that I must love him in his radically changed form. I must let go of my first Anthony in order to accept and love this new and different one.

I still struggle with depression when thinking of what my first son might have had. I imagine I always will. There are times that come upon me suddenly, particularly in the cool fall air, when I vividly recall moments that he and I had together. These moments squeeze my heart and take my breath away. Other moments, as when I run into a former friend of his, tug on me and make me wonder how Anthony might look, act or sound had he not suffered his accident. There are the inevitable events, like weddings of his same-age cousins and schoolmates which remind me that he will never have a wife, father a child, be a lover. I have to stop myself from wondering what his life would look like now.

I would be lying if I said I was over my loss. I'm not. I never will be.

But I am no longer on a mission to make Anthony as he was before. I have come to love my second son, accepting his disabilities. I now recognize that we share roles. Sometimes he is teacher and I am student in the school of our lives. As I observe, I learn. To him, life is simple. He needs food, shelter and love. He lives in the present, never worrying about the past or the future, what he has or doesn't have. He takes joy in being with his family and his few friends.

I continue to learn from those who surround me. Alex, who has grown into a talented and beautiful, mature-for-her-age college student, challenges me to continually update my thinking. Ashley, who left us behind the day she got married, reminds me through her absence to be a more attentive father, husband and uncle. Jeni, who now works with us, supports our business and family and helps me to value the people upon whom I depend. Steven, who Jeni adopted several years ago from Guatemala, teaches me to see the world through the fresh eyes of a young child. Linda, who walks with me arm-in-arm, works tirelessly and points the direction, as we grow our family, our business, our lives.

And Anthony, who is now in his twenties, reminds me regularly that being "on the right side of the dirt" is sufficient cause for happiness.

"Courage does not always roar. Sometimes courage is the quiet voice at the end of the day saying, 'I will try again tomorrow.'"
—MARY ANNE RADMACHER

TOOLBOX

Takeaways for Living through Crisis

Linda's 10
Coping Strategies for Crisis

1. Recruit and accept help and emotional support through family and friends. Do not try to weather the crisis alone.

2. Confide in your primary physician.

3. Be positive. Be proactive. Your attitude will contribute greatly to the outcome. Educate yourself and be involved as much as possible.

4. Recognize that "This too shall pass." You will have a "normal" life again, although it may never be as it was.

5. Find your mental "get-away" for particularly traumatic moments. Example: Envision yourself floating on calm water. Block out all distractions and center yourself.

6. Focus on others. Do not internalize. Who else needs your help during this crisis? How can you help those around you?

7. Stay busy. This is a bad time to be idle. Don't sit home alone.

8. Exercise regularly. Walk, run, bicycle thirty minutes every other day. The endorphins released will help you mentally and emotionally. Your sleep will improve. Your body will be stronger and you will feel more in control.

9. Sleep. Get a good night's sleep. Your body and brain need the recuperation time. If you are exhausted, you will be less effective at a critical time.

10. Eat well. Eat well-balanced meals, lots of fruits and vegetables, good proteins and complex carbohydrates. Your body and mind are in a state of hyper-stress. They need useful nutrients, not chemicals, processes and additives that sap your strength.

Finally, you will have moments that you can't avoid. Find a place; mine was in the closet, where you can really cry. Let it come. But set a limit, perhaps 4–5 minutes. Afterward move on. Do not dwell.

Dear Friend,

While Anthony was in the hospital, I talked to nurses, therapists, doctors, social workers and parents of other patients constantly. I was a novice who had to learn how to care for and rehabilitate a physically complicated child, so I asked questions of these people, who had experience and knowledge that I lacked.

From day one, I was as active as possible in his care and I learned to do everything the nurses and therapists did for my son while he was in the hospital, and later, when he returned to school. What these people taught me along the way was invaluable and their tutelage, referrals and insight have enhanced the quality of Anthony's life and ours as a family. Your loved one will benefit greatly if you can tap into the experienced people hospital and school environments offer, if you can find the energy to be actively involved in therapy and patient care, and if you can find a fun way to incorporate tasks into life at home.

I have provided information about agencies and pro-grams that offer various types of useful services. I hope you will investigate a few of them even if you don't see an immediate connection. You may be surprised upon discovering the width and depth of their offerings. At the very least, they might refer you on to another agency. Anthony is now involved in programs from several sources and each enhances the quality of his life.

Having worked with insurance companies, hospitals, schools and government agencies closely for more than a decade, I have found that I am most productive when I follow these guidelines:

- Try to work with the doctors, nurses, therapists, teachers, social workers and case managers with a "team" type of mentality—use "we" instead of "you" or "I." Offer to help whenever possible. Be polite and positive.

- Listen carefully. Don't be afraid to ask the tough questions or for clarification when you don't understand something.

- Take notes during all your phone interviews and meetings. You will then be able to reference important names, phone numbers and dates at a later time.

- If possible, use email when communicating in person is not practical. Copy yourself. This allows you to keep a "paper" trail. Email is also a good tool for summarizing a meeting, listing action steps and noting who is responsible for doing what and when. The "Reply to All" option is an excellent way to keep a team informed and up to date.

- Be persistent. Follow up regularly to ensure your case is moving forward.

- Be appreciative of the efforts these people make on your behalf. They are often overworked and underpaid. Thank them regularly.

Warmest regards,
Linda Cole

Alphabetical Directory
of Resources

Brain Injury Association of America (BIAA)

The Brain Injury Association of America (BIAA) is the leading national organization serving and representing individuals, families and professionals who are touched by a life-altering, often devastating, traumatic brain injury (TBI). Together with its network of more than 40 chartered state affiliates, as well as hundreds of local chapters and support groups across the country, the BIAA provides information, education and support to assist the 3.17 million Americans currently living with traumatic brain injury and their families. If you or someone you love has sustained a brain injury, please call the Brain Injury Association of America.

Many areas have a local branch of the BIAA that provides meetings, seminars and support for the individual and for families. To find the location nearest you, open the national website below, click on the State Offices tab, click on your state website, and then click on Support Group Listing.

(800) 444-6443
www.biausa.org

Children's Hospitals & Family Resource Centers

One of the many Children's Hospitals should be your first point of contact for issues relating to those under the age of eighteen. Most of the Children's Hospitals across the U.S. offer in-patient and community services through their Family Resource Centers. These centers provide a wide variety of useful services, including parent resources, parent-to-parent networks and support groups, information on health, wellness and psychosocial issues, homework support, assistance for out of town families, tips on working with your child's school, access to computers and internet, etc. Children's Hospitals social services department is the best source for children's services and for families in crisis.

Type Children's Hospital into your search engine window to find the closest location.

The Dougy Center

The Dougy Center was the first center in the United States to provide peer support groups for grieving children. The center has served over 20,000 children, teens and families since 1982. The National Center provides support and training locally, nationally and internationally to individuals and organizations seeking to assist children in grief.

The Dougy Center is supported solely through private support from individuals, foundations and companies, and receives no state or federal funding. The Dougy Center does not charge a fee for its services.

Locate The Dougy Center website through your internet browser. See Grief Resources.
(866) 775-5683
www.dougy.org

Facebook Group:
Mothers and Fathers with Disabled Children

An informal and interactive site for communicating with other parents/caregivers on Facebook, a free social utility that connects people around the world. Mothers and Fathers with Disabled Children is a forum for pertinent discussion and a place to get real-life-experience solutions and opinions about issues related to disabled children and families. The following link takes you to the Facebook site. Once registered and on your own personal site, type "Mothers and Fathers . . ." into the search window at the top of the page.
www.facebook.com

Feeding America

Feeding America is the nation's leading domestic hunger-relief charity. The organization's mission is to feed America's hungry through a nationwide network of member food banks and engage our country in the fight to end hunger. Each year, the Feeding America network provides food to more than 37 million low-income people facing hunger in the United States, including more than 14 million children and nearly 3 million seniors.

Feeding America's network of more than 200 food banks serves all 50 states, the District of Columbia and Puerto Rico, securing and distributing more than 2.5 billion pounds of food and grocery products annually. Those member food banks support approximately 63,000 local charitable agencies and 70,000 programs, which provide food directly to individuals and families in need. Because this organization is on the "front line," some of the local chapters have extended outreach services to provide clothing and shelter.

To find the location nearest you, open the website below and enter your zip code into the Food Bank Locator search box.

(800) 771-2303
www.feedingamerica.org

Medicaid

Medicaid is a government run health insurance program that helps five broadly defined groups including children, pregnant women, adults with dependent children, individuals with disabilities, and those age 65 and older.

Medicaid eligibility is determined by each state, using guidance provided by the federal government. Generally the program is reserved for America's poorest individuals, including children, who are considered without assets. Type "Medicaid" and your state into your search engine window.

National Association of State Directors of Developmental Disabilities (NASDDDS)

The National Association of State Directors of Developmental Disabilities Services (NASDDDS) is a nonprofit organization, established in 1964, to improve and expand public services to people with intellectual and other developmental disabilities. The NASDDDS's mission is to assist member state agencies in building person-centered systems of services and supports for people with developmental disabilities and their families.

To find the location nearest you, open the website below and click on your state shown on the map. Once the site opens up, click on your state's name. There you will find contact information.
(703) 683-4202
www.nasddds.org/MemberAgencies/index.shtml

National Council on Independent Living (NCIL)

NCIL helps disabled individuals find housing that will allow them to live independently. The organization also helps to transition those in high school into adult environments and, if it can't provide the needed services, it will refer you to another agency.

The National Council on Independent Living is the longest-running national cross-disability, grassroots organization run by and for people with disabilities. Founded in 1982, NCIL represents thousands of organizations and individuals including: Centers for Independent Living (CILs), Statewide Independent Living

Councils (SILCs), individuals with disabilities, and other organizations that advocate for the human and civil rights of people with disabilities throughout the United States.

To find the location nearest you, open the website below and click on your state.

(877) 525-3400

www.ilru.org/html/publications/directory/index.html

National Dissemination Center for Children with Disabilities (NICHCY)

NICHCY is pleased to offer you a wealth of information on disabilities. NICHCY stands for the National Dissemination Center for Children with Disabilities. We serve the nation as a central source of information on:

- Disabilities in infants, toddlers, children, and youth,
- IDEA, which is the law authorizing special education,
- No Child Left Behind (as it relates to children with disabilities), and
- Research-based information on effective educational practices.
- Feel free to communicate with us in English or Spanish. We're here, we're listening, and it would be our pleasure to help you.

(800) 695-0285 (Voice/TTY)

www.nichcy.org

National Suicide Prevention Lifeline

Are you, or is someone you know, in crisis? Please call **(800) 273-TALK** Are you feeling desperate, alone or hopeless? Call the National Suicide Prevention Lifeline at **(800) 273-TALK (8255)**, a free, 24-hour hotline available to anyone in suicidal crisis or emotional distress. Your call will be routed to the nearest crisis center to you.

- Call for yourself or someone you care about
- Free and confidential
- A network of more than 140 crisis centers nationwide
- Available 24/7

Social Workers and Your Local Hospital

One of your best referral sources, social workers know the programs available and can put you in touch with services that are relevant to your situation. Call your local hospital and ask to speak with a social worker. The social services department will usually take you on as a Community Referral at no charge even if you are not a patient.

United Way

United Way is a worldwide network in 45 countries and territories, including nearly 1,300 local organizations in the U.S. It advances the common good, creating opportunities for a better life for all, by focusing on the three key building blocks of education, income and health. The

United Way movement creates long lasting community change by addressing the underlying causes of problems that prevent progress in these areas. LIVE UNITED is a call to action for everyone to become a part of the change.

To find services, visit the website below and enter the word "help" into the Search the Site box or telephone The Call Center at 2-1-1.

2-1-1
www.liveunited.org

For a more current and extensive
listing of resources,
please visit our website
www.ResurrectingAnthony.com

Tell Us Your Story
of Personal Courage!

Inspire Others with Your Story
of Overcoming Adversity

Have you made it through a personal crisis of your own? Have you helped someone else? We'd love to hear how you did it.

This is your chance to help others and make a real difference in the world. Share the experience and insights that helped you overcome your challenge so that others may benefit from your wisdom.

We're developing The Personal Courage Series® to publish books that contain short stories that address a specific life crisis such as loss of a partner; struggling with medical issues like Alzheimer's, cancer and others; and confronting emotional and psychological conditions like eating disorders, addiction and abuse. Get your name in print or remain anonymous—it's your choice—just help us to help others!

Don't worry if you aren't a writer. We will help. We can even write your story for you. For guidelines, a complete list of topics, or to submit your story of Personal Courage, please visit our website at www.ResurrectingAnthony.com or contact us:

Alexandra Publishing LLC
P.O. Box 42122, Cincinnati Ohio 45242
Phone: (513) 376-8782
Fax: (513) 791-3468

Personal contact information is confidential and will not be sold or traded.

Your purchase makes a difference.
10% of all profits donated to
Freestore Foodbank.